YOUR HOLISTIC BUSINESS RECIPE

YOUR HOLISTIC BUSINESS RECIPE

Essential Ingredients for a Sustainable Health and Well-Being Business

By Helen Harding

AEON

First published in 2020 by
Aeon Books
PO Box 76401
London W5 9RG

British Library Cataloguing in Publication Data

A C.I.P. for this book is available from the British Library

ISBN-13: 978-1-91280-712-3

Typeset by Medlar Publishing Solutions Pvt Ltd, India
Printed in Great Britain

www.aeonbooks.co.uk

This book is dedicated to you and your ability to create a sustainable, thriving complementary practice, therapy or coaching business. I know you can do this!

CONTENTS

ABOUT THE AUTHOR   xv

CHAPTER ONE
Introduction   1
   This book is for you if…   2
   Common myths about building a successful practice   3
   Procrastination will kill your practice   5
   Imperfect action   5
   How to use this book   6

CHAPTER TWO
Setting You Up for Success   9
   Confidence to practice   9
      EXERCISE: Confidence boosters   10
   Build your support network   10
      EXERCISE: Your supporters   11
   Empathy includes self-empathy   11
   Build your resilience   12

EXERCISE: Feel-good activities   13
Finding time   13
Setting boundaries   14

CHAPTER THREE
Reality Check   19
   Reflection   19
   Mind map yourself   21

CHAPTER FOUR
Creating Your Dream Practice   25
      EXERCISE: Your why   26
   Setting your vision   27
      What is a vision?   27
      EXERCISE: Creating your vision   27
      Dreaming big   28
      Setting your vision   28

CHAPTER FIVE
Setting Up Your Business   31
   Naming your business   31
      Working under your name   32
      Creating a business name   32
   Setting up a practice   33
      Business structure   33
      HM Revenue & Customs   34
      Professional body   34
      Data protection   34
      Insurance   35
      Terms and conditions   35
      Client agreements and supplier contracts 36
      Health and Safety Executive   36
      Business bank account   36
   Finding suitable premises   36
      Home practice   37
      Single discipline and multi-discipline clinics 38
      Rented rooms   39
      Online services   39
   Practitioner safety   39

Understanding your finances   41
Your cost of living   41
EXERCISE: Your cost of living   41
Business money   42
Simple accounts   42
Building in buffers   43
EXERCISE: Building in buffers   44

CHAPTER SIX
Creating Your Personal Brand   47
You are your brand   47
Authentic marketing   48
EXERCISE: Marketing yourself authentically   49
Building connections with your story   49
EXERCISE: Your story   50
Creating your brand   51
Positioning yourself   52
EXERCISE: Talking points   53
Logo and style   53
DIY logo   53
Create your colour palette   54
Create your brand guidelines   54
Profile photo   54

CHAPTER SEVEN
Your Clients   57
What is a generalist?   57
Choosing a niche   58
EXERCISE: Finding your niche   59
Six-month commitment   60
Understanding your clients   60
EXERCISE: Making research calls   61
Online research   62

CHAPTER EIGHT
Your Services and Products   65
Packaging your services and products   66
Digital products   66
Create your packages   67

Minimum viable product   69
Seven steps to creating your MVP   70
Creating physical products   70
Affiliate marketing   71
Retail   72

CHAPTER NINE
Setting Your Prices   73
        EXERCISE: Information for setting your prices   74
How much should you charge?   75
Working out your pricing   75
Setting budgets   76
Forecasting   77
"You are too expensive!"   77
Should you work for free?   78
        EXERCISE: Own your value   79

CHAPTER TEN
Marketing Basics   83
    Always ask "Why?"   84
    Creating your marketing message   85
        EXERCISE: Your simple marketing message   85
        Deeper messaging   86
        EXERCISE: Crafting your deeper message   86
    Case studies and testimonials   87
        What to include   87
        Collecting case studies and testimonials   88
        Have a process   89
        What if I do not have testimonials?   89
    Offering freebies   89
        Handling requests for free work   91
        Helping people for free without draining yourself 91
    Building a business with conversation   92
    How much marketing should you do?   93

CHAPTER ELEVEN
Making Marketing Fun   95
        EXERCISE: What is fun for you?   96
    Marketing to your strengths   96

EXERCISE: Your communication strengths   97
Activities based on strengths   97
Communicating with your ideal clients   97
Keep it simple   98

CHAPTER TWELVE
Selling from the Heart   101
  Helpful marketing   102
  Making offers   102
  Follow-up   102
  Tell clients the next step   103
  Understanding your client journey   104
    EXERCISE: Map out your client journey   105

CHAPTER THIRTEEN
Marketing Recipe   107
  The simple plan   108
  Yearly overview   109
    EXERCISE: Your yearly overview plan   110
  Creating your recipe   111
   Hot leads   112
   Warm leads   113
   Cold leads   113
   EXERCISE: Hot, warm, and cold leads   114
   Your recipes   114
   Testing   115
   Example of a recipe with ingredients and steps 116
   EXERCISE: Your marketing recipe   117

CHAPTER FOURTEEN
Ethical Marketing Activities: Traditional   119
  Personal outreach (hot leads)   119
  Business cards (hot, warm, and cold leads)   120
  Word of mouth marketing (hot and warm leads)   121
   Building a referral system   122
  Standing out in your local community (warm and cold leads)   123
   Good quality signage   123
   Utilising physical space   124
   Community events   124

Handwritten cards (hot leads)   125
Giving talks (warm and cold leads)   126
Networking (warm and cold leads)   127
Collaborations (hot, warm, and cold leads)   129
Practice leaflet (cold leads)   130
   How to create a leaflet that works   131
Public relations (cold leads)   131
Setting up a stand (cold leads)   133
   Making your stand, stand out   134

CHAPTER FIFTEEN
Ethical Marketing Activities: Website   135
  Website (hot, warm, and cold leads)   135
   Start simply   137
   Refresh your existing website   138
   About page   139
   Search engine optimisation   140
   Marketing your website   141
  Content creation (hot, warm, and cold leads) 142
   Blogging   142
   Infographics   142
   Podcasting   143
   Video   144

CHAPTER SIXTEEN
Ethical Marketing Activities: Online   147
  Email list (hot and warm leads)   147
  Email newsletter (hot and warm leads)   149
  Social media (hot, warm, and cold leads)   150
  Google My Business Page (cold leads)   152
  Online directories (cold leads)   152
  Online advertising (cold leads)   153

CHAPTER SEVENTEEN
Marketing Lessons   157
  Copywriting basics   157
  Repurpose your marketing   159
  Finding inspiration   160
   EXERCISE: Content inspiration   162

Editorial calendar   162
Simple editorial calendar   164
EXERCISE: Your editorial calendar   165
Understanding what works   165
Briefing a designer   167
Eight steps to writing a brief   167

CHAPTER EIGHTEEN
Making it Happen   171
Focus   171
Simplify things   173
Start with simple   174
Declutter your to-do list   174
Get a good routine   175
Creating checklists   175
EXERCISE: Your checklists   176
Batching   176

CHAPTER NINETEEN
When the Going Gets Tough   179
Success saboteurs   180
Perfectionism   180
Procrastination   183
EXERCISE: Procrastination awareness   184
Shiny marketing syndrome   184
Putting the needs of others first   185
EXERCISE: Personal boundaries   186
Scarcity mindset   186
EXERCISE: Creating an abundant mindset   187
Stopping the sabotage   187

CHAPTER TWENTY
Over to You!   191

CHAPTER TWENTY ONE
Resources   193
Books—marketing   193
Books—mindset and productivity   195
Internet resources and links   196

Advertising Standards Authority (ASA)   196
Companies House   196
British Chambers of Commerce (BCC)   196
The Federation of Small Businesses (FSB)   196
Google My Business (GMB)   197
Government services and information (United Kingdom)   197
Health and Safety Executive (HSE)   197
Information Commissioners Office (ICO)   198
Local Authority (LA) website   198
Medicines and Healthcare products Regulatory Agency (MHRA)   198
Princes Trust   198

BIBLIOGRAPHY AND REFERENCES   199
  Websites   200

ACKNOWLEDGEMENTS   203

ABOUT THE AUTHOR

Helen Harding is both a complementary practitioner and a chartered marketer. She spent over 20 years working in marketing and business before following her interest in personal development. Within four years Helen was earning a living as a practitioner, working three days a week but earning the equivalent of a full-time salary.

Her passion for marketing and business never left her, and she recognised that these were the areas her fellow practitioners struggled with most. She started to support her colleagues, helping them to build their own businesses, their way.

Helen's unique approach blends her skills in personal development, marketing, and business, specifically to support other complementary practitioners, therapists and coaches. She has had the opportunity to lecture at a university on business skills and planning, tutored and supervised student practitioners, and developed and implemented business structures for private practices and colleges teaching complementary practitioners.

CHAPTER ONE

Introduction

It saddens me when amazing complementary practitioners, therapists and coaches fail to reach their full potential or even stop practising altogether. When I trained as a practitioner there were 60 of us all excited about making a difference in the world. Ten years on, only a handful of us are still working as practitioners. Having spoken with hundreds from many different disciplines, there are common themes as to why they struggle:

- Limited business and marketing skills
- Lacking the confidence to practice
- Lack of ongoing support

I want to change this! This book is the starting point to help you flourish as a practitioner and help those clients who are waiting for your unique approach to health and well-being. It is all about creating a thriving, sustainable practice on your terms. There is work to do and it will be challenging at times. It is not about following yet another system, but about creating your own recipe, one where you are more likely to do the work because it is tailored to you, and will therefore ultimately succeed.

In the UK, we are living in a time where members of our government are calling for complementary, traditional and natural medicine to rescue our National Health Service (NHS) from financial crisis

According to a report by the All Party Group for Integrated Healthcare (2018), the rising costs to the health system require a whole-person approach to health delivery which focuses on prevention and tackles the root cause of illness. It concluded we should make greater use of natural, traditional and complementary therapies, which are widely used for a variety of conditions. There is a huge under-utilised resource of therapists which could work in collaboration with conventional medicine to improve patient outcomes and ease the burden on the NHS. This is great news for your practice!

There are literally hundreds of ways you can market yourself and your services, but you cannot do them all. In my experience, successful practitioners have a clear way of attracting clients: they build strong relationships and have a simple way to deliver their products and services. I will guide you through the business basics you need to create stable foundations on which to build your practice. I look at what you need to set up in your business first, where to start with your marketing, and how to begin developing your own marketing recipe which you can deliver consistently to attract clients.

This is your business and you are at the heart of it. I will help you work out what kind of business you want to create, how you like to work, and with whom.

This book is for you if...

You work in health and well-being as a complementary or alternative medicine (CAM) professional, therapist or coach and want to make a difference by building a sustainable business using marketing techniques that suit you and your business model. Whether you are new, or struggling, or if you are overwhelmed by the number of choices available and do not know where to start to grow your business, this book will seek to guide you through the process.

Get rich quick schemes and blueprints may work for the creator, but it does not mean they will work for you. The designer may have found their way of building a successful business, but there is no "one-size-fits-all" approach. What works for you will be completely different from what works for me, or the online expert claiming to have "the answer". The constant barrage of "work longer, work harder, work faster, work better" just leads to frustration, disappointment, and forgotten dreams. Unfortunately, practitioners often get disheartened when they cannot achieve the promised results or stick to the dictated routines after buying into the promise of overnight success.

By creating your own recipe for your business and selecting the right ingredients that work to your strengths and fit with your values, you can succeed where others fail. This book is about building your business without selling your soul or burning yourself out in the process. It is a pragmatic guide to help you build a sustainable health and wellbeing business, your way.

Depending on your discipline, you may call the people you work with patients or clients. For consistency, I refer to them as clients throughout this book and likewise I will refer to you as a practitioner.

Common myths about building a successful practice

Once qualified, clients will come. This would be wonderful but unfortunately it is a long way from the reality of building a thriving, sustainable practice. You must let people know you exist, and how you can help them. You must learn how to market yourself effectively and make offers to prospective clients.

If I do another course/qualification, clients will come. This is procrastination. No matter how much you learn, there will always be more to know. One more course or qualification will not help you find clients. You need to start where you are and do the best with what you have. You can always add to your knowledge in the future, but you must get started. Finding paying clients is your priority if you want to thrive as a practitioner.

The Universe will answer. I believe in the Law of Attraction, but I also believe you must make it happen, you cannot just sit back and wait. By all means set out your intentions to the Universe but demonstrate how serious you are by the actions you take.

It is impossible to be successful. This is a huge limiting belief for many practitioners. You are qualified, you do amazing work, but you are still scraping around trying to find clients. Yes, it is hard work to be successful and have a sustainable business, but it is not impossible. Look around at some of the amazing, successful practitioners you admire to see what is possible with the right recipe.

The magic formula. There are many people out there pedalling their system, blueprint or formula as "the" answer to building a business. Unfortunately, there is no one-size-fits-all solution that will work for everyone. How you market yourself will be different depending on you, your clients, your resources, and the stage you are at in your business. You have to develop your own recipe and build your business your way for it to work for you.

I do not need to know my numbers. Accounts may not be your thing and you may choose to outsource your book-keeping and accounts. You do however, need to understand and track your basic numbers to be able to make good decisions for your practice.

I can do everything myself. As with every small business owner, you wear a lot of hats. Whilst you may be able to stumble your way through all sorts of jobs, there is a lot you should not be doing.

When you start out, you do more than you should because you probably do not have the budget to get the help you need. As you grow, your time is your biggest asset and there will be certain tasks only you can do. There will also be lots of tasks you should be outsourcing to professional services.

Practitioners often shy away from using marketing service providers such as photographers, copywriters, or designers in favour of doing things themselves. If you are a medical herbalist, why would a client come to see you instead of visiting their local health shop? It is because they will get superior healthcare, knowledge and service. So, why would you design your own leaflet instead of hiring a graphic designer once you can afford it?

I do not need help. Working as a practitioner can be a lonely journey and you need help to thrive. If you are very independent and used to digging deep and battling through it can be tough to ask for help. Working solo, you are too close to what you are doing and you can easily make some pretty costly mistakes. Having a team of supporters will help keep you focused and moving forward with your business.

There is too much competition! Practitioners often feel discouraged because there are so many others out there competing for new clients. This can knock their confidence and they end up feeling they will never be successful.

If there are others successfully offering a solution to the same problems as you, consider it a good thing. This shows that they are solving a problem that people need help with and, more importantly, are willing to pay for it. This means your business is viable.

It is true, there are many, many different practitioners out there. But there is one thing many have in common, they do not stand out!

So many of the practitioners you view as competition ignore marketing. They do not build their profile to attract the right clients and just spend time waiting in the hope that the phone will ring. The only reason they are visible to you is because you are consciously looking for and therefore, noticing them.

Procrastination will kill your practice

Procrastination comes in many forms and will stop you in your tracks and prevent you from ever getting your business off the ground. Be aware of your favourite ways to procrastinate. A few common forms are:

Waiting for something to happen. Putting off things until something happens is a sure-fire way of never getting going. Once the first thing is achieved something else quickly replaces it.

Waiting until you are ready. The reality is you are never ready! At some point you must take the leap, or you will always be waiting and watching everyone overtake you.

Perfection. This saboteur is something I have struggled with over the years and see in many of my clients. Why do we strive so hard for something unattainable? Seeking perfection is a guaranteed way to never feel good enough and to stop you from achieving your potential and helping the people you want to. You can find more on "perfection" in Chapter 19, When the going gets tough.

Fear of failure. You spend your time imagining how you will fail dramatically and how shameful it will be. People will say "I told you so" and you will be found out for who you really are. Running these thoughts repeatedly will keep you from ever being successful.

Imperfect action

Taking action is the difference between those who are successful and those who plan to be, but never quite get there. It is very easy to get caught up in the dreaming and planning stages of your business and before you know it you are a month past your initial deadline and still have not started.

It is time to start doing! Imperfect action is the remedy to procrastination. The skill of getting things done supersedes talent and intelligence when setting up and marketing your business. Cultivating this skill will help you build a sustainable and thriving practice. Taking action requires you to face your fears and find the courage to move forward. The rewards can be outstanding and you will be doing the work you were born to do. Are you ready to get started?

How to use this book

Buy yourself a beautiful notebook or create a file on your phone or computer, you need something to keep all your notes and ideas together. Ultimately, you want a go-to reference point for your business where you note your thoughts and decisions and can refer to it as you need to.

Start from where you are, right now. It does not matter where you are in the year, you will benefit from checking you have the right foundations for your business in place and creating your own special marketing recipe.

Give yourself time and space to do the work. You will not get it all done in one sitting but that is okay, your business will always be a work in progress. It is however important to build in regular time to work on your business rather than constantly working in it. This is where the magic happens and the opportunities will present themselves.

Work through the different sections of this book and if one does not apply to you skip it and move onto the next one.

Have your notebook or file at hand so you can refer to and add to it regularly as you do the work. Your recipe will constantly be evolving and as you develop you want to capture your ideas and decisions as you go.

As you work through the sections, we will identify some of the common mindset issues that may threaten to sabotage your progress. There may be times when you need to call on your favourite technique to help you work through the challenge, whether it is journaling, meditation, Neuro Linguistic Programming (NLP), Emotional Freedom Technique (EFT), visualisation or something else. Do what works for you!

There is no one approach that fits everyone, but I have included a few of my favourite tips throughout this book to help you flow through the challenges.

If you find yourself particularly stuck in one area, I urge you to work through it with a coach or practitioner as they will assist you in finding a faster resolution than struggling on your own.

CHAPTER TWO

Setting You Up for Success

Whilst I hope you will find yourself flowing through the process of setting up and running your business, life is not always like that! There will be challenging times but having your support systems in place will help you navigate them as they happen and come out stronger on the other side. I will cover creating your support systems in this chapter.

Confidence to practice

If you struggle with confidence when you think about working with clients, you are not alone. It is perfectly normal for new (and experienced) practitioners to wobble from time to time. The good news is confidence will come with experience; it does not come with doing yet another course or waiting until you are ready.

Confidence to practice is knowing you will do your best in any given situation and be able to handle challenges that come your way. Confidence does not mean you will know everything, but that you can think clearly and act appropriately to make the best recommendations for your clients. It is also having the confidence to recognise when you are not the right person for the client or when you do not have the appropriate experience or skills to work with them.

> ### EXERCISE: Confidence boosters
>
> Grab your notebook and answer these questions to create your list of confidence boosters. Refer to them at times when you need a lift to reinforce why you are the best practitioner for your clients:
>
> - Why do you do what you do?
> - What have you achieved that qualifies you to practice?
> - What are your strengths as a practitioner?
> - What are the qualities you get complimented for?
> - What are the great things your clients say about you?

Build your support network

When you train you are surrounded by colleagues and friends. Everyone is excited about the future and building their dream practice. The reality of working in health and well-being can be very different. The feeling of isolation can creep in when you start to build your business. You become aware of all the different aspects of creating a business and just how many of those result in you working on your own. It can be a very lonely journey at times.

Having a great support network around you will act as a buffer and help you to be resilient through challenging times. Being able to confide in a good friend, a suitable mentor, or peer in your professional life will allow you to share concerns, gain support, and discover solutions in a safe environment.

Become business buddies with a colleague, someone who understands what you do and is at a similar stage in their business. A larger version of this is to create a peer support group (often referred to as a mastermind) with other practitioners. It does not matter if they do not work within the same discipline as you, look for practitioners with a similar business model and experience of working with clients. Paid masterminds run by business and marketing specialists are available and are a great option to get professional support at a fraction of the cost of hiring your own business coach. A business buddy or a mastermind group will be there to celebrate your wins and support you through the challenges you face. You can bounce ideas around together and be kept accountable.

Larger support groups are available in online communities and include paid memberships and free social media groups. There are some amazing communities out there, but you do need to choose wisely as they can be a big-time drain and easily become another way of procrastinating.

EXERCISE: Your supporters

In your notebook, list your go-to people who will cheer you on, help keep you motivated and give you a big hug when times are tough. These are the people you count on to listen but will also tell you the hard truth if you are out of alignment with your values.

Empathy includes self-empathy

Our relationship with our clients plays a crucial role in their journey to health and well-being. The time we spend really understanding and working with them hugely enhances the effectiveness of our work. An empathetic practitioner will put their clients at ease. To be able to consistently provide compassionate services you must be emotionally and physically healthy.

If you are running low in any of the following areas you are in danger of burning out. This will affect your ability to be an effective practitioner. At worst, it could totally stop you from being able to function or work.

Body. How well do you look after your body? Are you regularly making time to exercise or include movement into your schedule? Do you have a good, balanced diet that gives you the fuel you need? Are you filling your body full of toxins? Looking after your body will help you feel energised and full of vitality.

Stress. This is a huge problem and can cause debilitating symptoms including poor quality sleep, immune system issues, digestive issues and not being able to think clearly. By calming down the stress response, it is amazing how quickly changes can happen and your brain and body can return to balance.

Connection. Feeling lonely and disconnected from others will deplete you. As humans we crave connection so make sure you have a community of people you can turn to where you feel connected and supported.

Purpose. Having a purpose in life will keep you motivated and move you forward. Reminding yourself of your purpose will fire up your energy and help you find the passion to do the work you find more challenging.

Environment. Do your different environments feel harmonious? If they are out of sync with you they will deplete your energy. If there are small practical steps you can take to improve your environment it is well worth the effort.

If there are bigger jobs you cannot do anything about immediately, clear your head of thoughts about it by writing them down and create a plan of action. This will free up your headspace from trying to remember and plan everything. Then use your chosen approach to work on accepting things as they are and letting go of any frustrations with where you currently are.

Changing your environment regularly and spending time in nature is a great way to recharge, especially if your home and work environments are a work in progress.

Build your resilience

Do what you can to cultivate your personal resilience. Setting up and running a business can be the most rewarding thing you do but it will also challenge you and test you to the limit. It will be your biggest personal development lesson ever!

Decide you are someone who thrives. No matter what happens, use life's challenges as stepping-stones rather than obstacles. When things do not go your way, reflect on them and understand the lesson you can learn from the situation. Build a strong belief that you can thrive and find evidence to support this. Remember times when you overcame something against all the odds and flourished. You can also use examples from friends, colleagues, and people you respect who are thriving.

Be flexible. Flexibility is a crucial part of resilience and by learning to be more flexible you will be better able to respond effectively in times of change. I love to think of water at times when I need to be flexible and flow through challenges. Water will always return to flow, no matter what obstacles present. Put a rock in a stream and it will find a way around or over it, freeze water and it will thaw, heat it and it will turn into steam which will turn back into water again.

Decide to be an optimist. This is a habit you can adopt relatively quickly. Start practising gratitude and noticing what is already working in your life and work. What inspires and excites you? What do you love doing? This does not mean ignoring what is not working; it is understanding that setbacks are transient. You can combat the challenges you face and move on.

Take good care of yourself. Focus on building your self-care skills, especially when things are less than perfect. Make time for the activities you enjoy and give yourself full permission to take care of your own needs. You cannot do your best work if you feel tired and stressed, you must place yourself at the top of your priority list.

EXERCISE: Feel-good activities

Create a list of feel-good activities that take no longer than 15 minutes, for example meditating, walking barefoot in the grass, phoning a friend, reading a magazine, gardening, or yoga stretches. Choose things which light you up and give you a quick boost. List them in your notebook and if you need a quick recharge, pick one and do it.

Finding time

Time is your most precious resource and needs to be valued. It is something everyone complains about not having enough of, but there are always ways to reclaim time with a little creativity. There are things you can do to either buy or create time which you can then invest in building your practice. These things do not have to be forever, but the more time you have to spend on developing your business and marketing it the faster it will take off (assuming you are working on the right things).

Employ help. This can be at home or within your business. Hiring a cleaner will give you back a few hours a week, or a bookkeeper if you hate doing your accounts, or a virtual assistant to help with your social media scheduling.

Delegate. Consider what tasks and chores can be delegated to others to reduce the number of items on your job list. Where can you get help from your family and friends?

Borrow from your down time. Think about the things you are willing to give up or reduce the time you spend on them to get your business up and running. Examples could be mindlessly watching TV, hobbies, socialising, or playing games on your phone. Whilst you definitely need time to relax and spend with people, we are only talking about borrowing time in the short term.

Let go of things. Again, this does not have to be forever but identify areas where time can be saved and redirected. What are you prepared to live without doing in return for making your business a success? A few ideas could be living with an overgrown garden, not ironing anything, or letting go of people who drain your time and energy.

> ## EXERCISE: Reclaiming time
>
> Grab your notebook and write down ideas for where you can claim back time to invest in building your business.
>
> - Where can you employ help?
> - What tasks can you delegate and to whom?
> - What downtime activities can you give up or reduce?
> - What can you let go of?

Setting boundaries

It is so tempting to always make yourself available especially if you are struggling to get enough clients, or just starting out. We have all been there, offering a late, last-minute evening appointment, when we really want to be winding down and having dinner with our family. But no, we are working, with a cold coffee and regretting our decision.

Saying yes can be the automatic response, but you have a choice. There is always a cost for saying yes, you are automatically saying no to something, or someone else. You have a finite amount of time and resources and you do not want to be in a situation where you regret it later.

Setting good boundaries will help to keep you grounded as a practitioner. They demonstrate clearly that you have the courage to respect yourself and value your work. Even when clients are not impressed, or happy with the situation, if they want to work with you they will be flexible. Setting boundaries helps your clients to understand the rules of engagement with you. It will set the expectations of what is appropriate in your relationship.

Respect the boundaries you set and if you say you do not work weekends, avoid responding to emails or texts on a Sunday night. To do otherwise tells your clients you work at the times you say you do not, which sends them mixed messages.

Whilst you love the work you do, you need to have space away from it. If people ask you for your professional opinion outside of work, gently divert them towards how they can work with you or find out more information. Boundaries work the other way too! When you are passionate about what you do you can find yourself trying to help people, when they have not asked for it. Sometimes people do not need you to have the solutions, they just want you to be a friend.

It is so much easier to feel compassionate towards your clients when you feel respected. If you feel people are taking advantage of your good nature, it can make working with them challenging. Clients who respect and honour your boundaries will help you to thrive as a practitioner and build a sustainable business.

EXERCISE: Setting your boundaries

Write down in your notebook your expectations for working with clients, you will be returning to these as you work through this book. Having a point of reference for what is acceptable will help you to communicate your boundaries when you are talking to people. They will also be included in your client agreement and advertised where appropriate, for example on your website and in your clinic.

TAKEAWAY

You are one person and you cannot do everything on your own. You need your support network and systems to help you flow through the challenges of building your business.

CASE STUDY

Name: Jenny Gebka
Discipline: Rehabilitation Pilates Instructor
Website: AdaptivePilates.co.uk

After a corporate career, Jenny retrained as a Rehabilitation Pilates Instructor. She helps people to regain their fitness after injury or illness. Jenny also supports those with conditions that make general Pilates classes unsuitable, to lead an active life.

Why did you decide to become a practitioner?

I have always been interested in how the body works. At school I was torn between a degree in Biochemistry and becoming a physiotherapist (I was advised to do the former!). Years later, when I was unable to work as I had to care for my elderly father, I realised this was my chance to re-train and go back to my original idea of helping people. The training fitted in with looking after Dad and kept me sane!

What is your vision for your business?

I would like to help as many people as possible to get the most out of their lives by being active. I have witnessed the devastation, the inability to do something as simple as walking has on folk, after seeing both my parents going through really tough physical issues in later life. I want to prevent such problems for others.

Working one-to-one is more satisfying than teaching in group classes or creating online videos, so I want to continue teaching Pilates on a personal basis. I love the intricacies of helping individuals overcome their particular challenges, something you cannot do if working with a group or remotely.

The business also needs to fit in with my life, even after my husband retires.

What are the most important things to date that have helped you grow your business?

1. Finding a mentor who is like-minded but has different skills has provided invaluable support when I have hit the inevitable tough times.

2. Building relationships with people who are enthusiastic about my work through networking or online. For example, a leader of a business networking group has promoted me during her networking sessions, supported a workshop I ran (bringing additional friends with her) and helped me to access other channels, such as a lady's group. I have also had referrals from other complementary practitioners who have experienced and liked my work.
3. Keeping an open mind to how I can deliver my services and taking every opportunity and evaluating it to see if it can be achieved and if it is viable.

With hindsight, is there anything you would have done differently?

Pilates is great, but I wish I had trained earlier as an actual physiotherapist all those years ago. That way the intense training would have sunk in easier and I would have helped so many more people by now! But you cannot live your life rueing any decision you have made!

What is next for your business?

As it stands, my income is limited by the time spent with the number of individuals I can fit into a day. I normally help my clients over a difficult patch, teach skills so they can look after themselves and ultimately, they overcome their issue and no longer need my services. At this point they are able to manage their original issues and will only come back to me if they have another issue (or have forgotten how to keep the original one at bay!). In order to grow my business, I therefore need to find various ways to earn an ongoing income. I cannot say too much at the moment, but I am currently looking at what I can do to motivate clients to remember the skills I have given them, to ensure they are able to keep doing whatever activities they most enjoy.

CHAPTER THREE

Reality Check

Before we start looking at what to do to take your business forward, we need to start with where you are right now with an honest reality check. It is especially important if you have found yourself on the same merry-go-round in your business year after year. You know, the one you swore you would get off but here you are, still going around and around. If you are new to your business you can still do this, but look at it but from the perspective of the resources available to you and how you think about certain areas of your business.

You will need your notebook to complete this section and it may take a while. The effort will be well worth it when you start growing your dream practice.

Reflection

Knowing how you have done over the last year will help you improve your results next year. Keep note of your thoughts and findings as you work through this section as you will need them to build on later. If you are just starting out, think what these different areas will be for you.

What aspects of your work did you love? Think about those things that really inspired you and put a great big smile on your face. What left you feeling really good about yourself and the work you do?

What ran like clockwork? Where did everything work seamlessly? Maybe it was your system for booking appointments or sharing social media updates, anything where things just worked as they should. You can use these examples as inspiration and apply the same strategies in other areas of your business to get those working brilliantly too.

Which bits did you absolutely hate? We all have certain tasks that we have to do in our business but would much rather avoid, I call them the "necessary evils". Consider exactly what you hate about these jobs, as this will provide you with ideas for making changes in the way you work.

What was a complete chore? Different from the bits you hate doing, there may be some things you find a chore and monotonous but do them anyway. Identifying these things will give you opportunities for finding better ways of doing them in the future whether it is utilising technology or delegating them to others.

What areas of your business have you really struggled with? Within your business, there will be things you really struggle with and these will zap a huge amount of your time and energy. Instead of struggling, work out what they are and find solutions to free you up and save your energy.

How do you feel about money? Some practitioners are happy to earn a fair wage whereas others shy away at the mention of the word "money". How do you feel about money? Are you happy to receive money in return for your services? Are you happy to ask for payment?

Where did your business income come from? List the services and products you currently offer, how many you sold, the price and how much you earned in total from them. This exercise will help you identify where your main income came from so make sure you include everything that generated money for your practice, even if it is not your main offering. You may have this information in your accounts or on a spreadsheet. If not, split your page into four columns and list the items, see the example in table one for ideas on what to include.

Table 1. Income streams

Item	Quantity sold	Price each	Total
1:1 client session	243	£80.00	£19,440.00
Workshop	36	£97.00	£3,492.00
Online course	52	£67.00	£3,484.00
Total income			**£26,416.00**

Are you earning enough personally? Is your business profitable, can you afford to pay yourself a living wage?

What marketing assets do you have? For example, do you have a website and an email list? Anything you can measure the numbers on, list them, for example how many people you have on your email list or how many followers you have on your social media platforms.

Do you have information packs, business cards, or leaflets? You can repurpose these for different uses, meaning you will not have to start from scratch each time.

What marketing activities did you do? List out all the marketing activities you have done over the last year and how often you did them. Make a note of which ones worked and brought new clients to your door and which ones did not.

Where do you need support in your business? Do you need a receptionist to take care of bookings and to greet clients? Do you need administration support? Do you need technical support for IT, marketing, or finance? These are the areas that if delegated will free you up to do more of what you love and less of what you are getting bogged down with.

Mind map yourself

This exercise can be an eye-opener and was an influencing factor in my decision to train as a practitioner many moons ago. I was stuck in a rut and while chatting to a friend about it over a coffee we decided to create mind maps of ourselves. It helped me understand different aspects of my life, the resources I had available and, importantly, it opened my eyes to options I had not even seen before.

Map out a picture of the different aspects of who you are, your resources and connections (see Figure 1). This will help you to identify different aspects and options you have available to you as you start to build your recipe. Like me, you may even find opportunities you had not considered before.

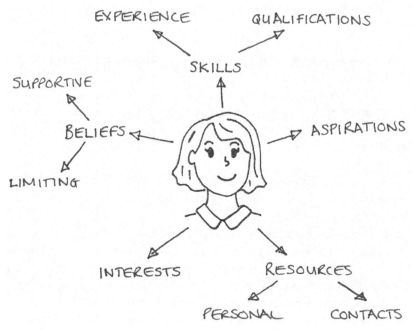

Figure 1: Mind map yourself.

SABOTEUR ALERT: Imposter syndrome and the comparison trap

These two tricky saboteurs may come into play as you review yourself and your business. They are responsible for keeping amazing practitioners playing small and never achieving their potential. If you find yourself:

- Feeling like an imposter or a fraud
- Constantly comparing yourself to others
- Being fearful of being exposed or found out
- Not feeling worthy

- Feeling that you are not good enough, or do not know enough
- Being a perfectionist and not finishing anything

You need to work on your mindset to help you move past them, so use your chosen technique or get support from your coach or practitioner. Also check out ideas in Chapter 19, When the going gets tough.

TAKEAWAY

Knowing exactly where you are may be scary but it will help you understand the choices available to you and make the right decisions for you and your business.

CHAPTER FOUR

Creating Your Dream Practice

When you are running your own business, it must make you happy. The whole point of working for yourself is, you get to write the rules. You pick what you do, whom you work with, and how you spend your time. If you are not happy with your practice, your clients will feel it and it will affect their experience of working with you.

Although your clients are who you serve, your business is built around you. It is about making sure your vision and values are fully represented, and that ultimately you work with your favourite clients.

Practitioners can fall out of love with their business if they have their priorities in the wrong order. Putting their clients first, their services second and themselves third does not make for a happy life. They are setting themselves up for failure as their own needs are not being met or prioritised properly.

Start with why you do what you do, what is it that makes you happy? What gets you up in the morning and excited about the day ahead? Considering the answers to these questions will help you create a vision for your life and business that works for you. It is important that your needs are being met in order to meet the needs of your clients.

By placing yourself at the heart of your business, you will start to determine who you should be working with and enjoy spending time with. You will have things in common with these people and probably have friends just like them.

Knowing what you stand for, what you believe in, and your cause will help you to communicate effectively. It will resonate with people who have similar beliefs. Over time, you will attract more of your favourite people to your practice and less of those who are not such a great fit. The aim is to do great work, but also to love what you do and be happy.

EXERCISE: Your why

Look up Simon Sinek's TEDx talk "Starting with Your Why", the videos can be found online. When you start with why you do something rather than trying to sell your service, your message will be more powerful and connect with the people you aim to serve.

Build on your mind map from the last chapter by adding what you stand for, what makes you happy, your values and vision (see Figure 2). This will help you to connect with your why. It will help you work out the things that make you, you and identify what you should be sharing in your marketing to connect with others who have the same passions as you.

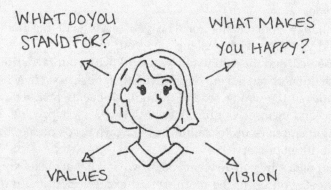

Figure 2: Mind map yourself.

Setting your vision

Having a clear vision will help you define what sort of business you should be building that works for you. It is one of the best things you can do for your business, but so often gets completely missed out. Without a vision, you will get carried along for the ride without knowing where you are going.

Many practitioners are driven by their passion for their discipline and helping people. They build a business similar to their peers because they think that is what is expected. Before they know it, they are floundering and do not know which way to turn.

If you have fallen into a working pattern that is not right for you, it is time to take a step back and start with the end in mind. You may not know exactly where you want to be in the future, and life changes constantly. Your vision is not set in stone, it will change and evolve with you over time.

What is a vision?

Your vision is how you want your life and business to look and feel in the future. Knowing what lifestyle you want will help you to create a business that supports it, in the right way for you.

Having a clear vision will give you direction and enable you to make good decisions without feeling overwhelmed. It will help you say yes to certain activities, and no to others. You will avoid getting side-tracked by the things you think you should be doing and instead, focus on the right things. Your vision will give you a sense of clarity in your life and business and help you achieve balance and order.

EXERCISE: Creating your vision

Give yourself space to take time out and to think clearly. Move to a different environment away from any distractions. Imagine your life and business in five or ten years from now and write down your answers to the following questions:

- What does an ideal day in your life look like?
- Who are the important people in your life?

- Where do you live?
- What is important to you?
- What are your hobbies?
- Who are the clients you are helping?
- How are you working with your clients?
- What hours and days are you working?
- Where are you working?
- How much are you earning?
- What other projects or charities are you involved in?
- How are you making yourself a priority?

Now you have a detailed description of how you want life to be. Spend some time imagining working in this way, does it feel right? Is it how you want to be living and working? Is this the ideal life and business for you?

Dreaming big

Does this vision live up to your big dreams? You know those secret, scary dreams you keep hidden because you do not believe they are really possible to achieve.

- Does your vision reflect how you really want to live or are you limiting your vision in any way?
- What fears do you have about allowing yourself to dream big?
- If there were no limits, what would change about your vision?

Now review your vision and make sure it includes space for your big dreams.

Setting your vision

Get creative and find a way of representing the vision that works for you. This is something you want to be able to refer to. It will act as a compass to help you navigate your way through the decisions you make in your life and business.
   A few suggestions are:

- Write your vision in your notebook or journal
- Draw it or create a piece of artwork to represent it
- Write phrases to describe it on sticky notes and stick them on your wall

- Create a vision board or collage
- Create a digital image or pinboard

Do whatever works for you. Find a way to represent exactly how you imagine yourself living and working. Now make sure you keep it in a place where you can see it as it will help to keep you on track and working towards your vision.

TAKEAWAY

You are at the heart of your business and your why and vision will act as a compass to keep you moving in the right direction.

CHAPTER FIVE

Setting Up Your Business

Naming your business

Deciding how to name your business is not always that simple. There are often fears around the decision like "using my name will make me look small" or "no-one will want to pay for my services if they know it is just me". There is a belief a business name will give you the appearance of being more professional, or more established, or bigger than you really are.

When considering a name, start with your vision for your business:

- Do you imagine continuing to work as a practitioner?
- Do you intend to build a business you can eventually sell?
- How will your business look in five years from now?

There is no right or wrong way to name your business and it can always be changed at a later date.

As humans, we relate to other humans and connect our experiences to faces and names. This is especially important when working in health and well-being, your relationship with your clients is based on you and the results they achieve from working with you. Even if you create a business name you need to be visible, and your name needs to be linked to it. You are the person your clients connect with and the person they trust.

Once you have decided your business name, make sure you buy a domain name and claim social media accounts to hold them for you. Where possible, use the same name and spelling format, keeping it simple for people to find you on different platforms.

Working under your name

Using your own name is the simplest way to work. You are creating a business and a brand based on you and the services you offer. Creating a personal brand with your name will help you to be visible and stand out from the competition. There is only one you, you are an original! It will make it easier to work out what your brand stands for and develop your voice as you can concentrate on just being yourself.

Working under your name will help you be flexible and make changes as your business evolves. Many of us change niche and/or discipline as we progress. Changing the focus of your business is easier with a personal brand as you will not have to start from scratch with your marketing each time you change direction.

Creating a business name

Giving your business a name is a good way of making you appear larger than you really are. It is useful if you are partnering with other practitioners, or your vision is to build a business bigger than just you, especially if you eventually plan to sell it. To make the business attractive to buyers it needs to be able to run without you. Therefore, distancing yourself from the business name is a good strategy.

Unless you are absolutely sure of your niche avoid naming your business after it. If you create a brand based on a niche and then change your mind there will be a lot of work and expense to make the required changes. For example, if you create a business around weight loss and call it "The Diet Queen" but then decide you want to work with menopausal women you will have to start from scratch with your marketing.

Setting up a practice

Once qualified, the reality of setting up a complementary practice can be a little daunting. It is scary how many practitioners fail to put in place the basic foundations designed to protect and support them.

The following considerations are provided as an overview of the business foundations you need in place based on the UK market. For complete transparency (I am not a solicitor or an accountant), the following information is based on my experience and research as a professional marketer and complementary practitioner. If you are struggling with any of these areas, please contact your legal or financial advisers to support you in making the right decision.

Business structure

This will define your legal responsibilities such as paperwork, taxes and how the profit is dealt with. It also defines your personal responsibility should the business make a loss.

Sole trader. Most practitioners are self-employed or sole traders. You are responsible for the running of your business; you bear the risks and take the profits or losses. As a sole trader you can employ staff, it does not mean you have to work alone.

Limited company. This is an organisation that you set up to run your business. A limited company is responsible in its own right for everything it does. Its finances are separate from your personal finances. Company directors are not personally responsible for debts the business cannot pay if it goes wrong, as long as they have not broken the law.

Partnership. Two or more people work together under a partnership agreement. The relationship is outlined in the agreement as well as the share of the risk and reward.

Social enterprise. An organisation that applies commercial strategies to maximise improvements in human and environmental well-being, rather than maximising profits for shareholders.

You can find out full information on UK business structures from HM Revenue & Customs (HMRC), the details are in Chapter 20, Resources. If you are outside the UK, research the legal business structures within your country.

HM Revenue & Customs

Registering with HMRC is a legal requirement in the UK, whatever your business structure. You are required to submit tax returns and pay National Insurance and Income Tax as part of running your business. Depending on the set up of your company, you may have other tax obligations. The HMRC website has full details and you can register there too.

Professional body

Your professional body will have a code of conduct you will have to work to. Depending on your discipline, you will also need to follow the guidelines of certain agencies such as the Medicines and Healthcare products Regulatory Agency (MHRA).

If you belong to more than one professional body, work on the side of caution and follow the one with the strictest regulations.

Data protection

The Information Commissioners Office (ICO) was set up to uphold information rights in the public interest. As a business owner, you have a responsibility to look after the data in your possession and this legislation will apply to you if you are in Europe, or if you are not but your clients, or prospective clients are. The General Data Protection Regulations (GDPR) and Data Protection Act 2018 (DPA 2018) cover your legal responsibilities to manage the data you hold. This is a very quick overview of the six principles:

- Look after personal data you hold in line with these principles and any other laws that apply, ensuring you do it in a fair and transparent way that is clear to the individual(s) involved.
- Communicate exactly what you are using the collected data for and use it for that reason only.
- Only collect the data you need for the purpose and nothing more.
- Be careful to collect accurate data and if there are any mistakes correct them quickly.
- Only keep the data while you need it and safely delete it when you do not.
- Be responsible in the way you hold data and take measures to keep it safe.

In the UK it is a legal requirement to register with the ICO, it takes minutes and is not expensive so do it now. See Chapter 20, Resources, for more details.

Insurance

We live in a society where everything comes with a warning. Insurance is there to protect you, your clients, and the public. In the event you have a complaint made against you, your insurer is there to advise and support you. It is crucial you are fully insured before you start working with clients, even if you are a student practitioner.

Some types of insurance are a legal requirement, it is important you have the right cover for your business. For example, if you work from home, your home contents insurance is unlikely to cover anything related to your business.

Different types of insurance include:

Professional indemnity insurance. This is to protect you if a claim is made against you for injury or loss resulting from the modality you practice. This needs to cover you, wherever you choose to work.

Product liability insurance. This is to protect you if a claim for injury or loss is made against you for a product you supply that is not covered by your professional indemnity insurance.

Public liability insurance. This will protect you if a claim for injury or loss is made against you by a third party. It is known as the "trip or slip" cover, so you are protected if an unforeseen accident occurred. If you work in a clinic they may have the cover, but this will only protect you if the owner is deemed legally liable.

Employer liability insurance. If you employ staff, this will protect you against claims from an employee.

Content and buildings insurance. This will protect you from theft and damage to, or from your property as it does with your house insurance at home.

Terms and conditions

Terms and conditions (T&Cs) are you setting out your metaphorical stall. These are the rules of engaging with you and are there to protect you and your business. If you cannot afford to employ a solicitor, you can join an association such as the Federation of Small Businesses (FSB) or Chamber of Commerce (BCC). You can also purchase T&Cs online but check the credentials of the company you are buying them from first.

Client agreements and supplier contracts

This will outline clearly what a client or supplier can expect when working with you and what you expect from them. It should cover everything about how you will manage your relationship, from preparation to timekeeping and payment. Everything should be clear and agreed in advance of you working together.

Health and Safety Executive

Health and Safety Executive (HSE) provides the regulatory framework for health and safety within the workplace. You are responsible for health and safety in your business. The laws are there to protect you, your employees, and the public from workplace dangers. If you have under five employees you do not have to write down your risk assessment and health and safety policy but it is good practice to have them whatever the size of your business.

Business bank account

Your business finances need to be kept separate from your personal finances. A business bank account will provide the functions you need to run your business efficiently, such as taking card payments.

Finding suitable premises

Researching new premises for your practice can be very exciting. There are so many different and interesting options available where you can work as a practitioner.

When you decide where you are going to work, you must ensure the location is fit for purpose before you sign any contracts. There are many different requirements for different disciplines, so just because somewhere is being used by other practitioners, it does not mean it will be suitable for you. Your professional body will have guidelines for your discipline outlined in their code of conduct so check that. For commercial properties you need to check whether it has the correct classification for use in relation to your discipline. Your Local Authority planning department will be able to advise you.

Additionally, you should speak to environmental health at your Local Authority to ensure that services supplied to the property are suitable for your intended purpose. They will also advise on whether you need to apply for a special treatment licence. This refers to both working from home and occupying a residential property.

Consider the following:

Location. How easy is it to find your clinic and get to it? Does it have different options for those travelling, such as good transport links or parking? Does the surrounding area meet your client's expectations? This will reflect on you and your service if the building or area is not well maintained.

Accessibility. If you are working with clients with mobility issues, are the premises and rooms suitable for their needs, for example do you have a ground floor office or clinic, and is it wheelchair accessible?

Overhearing. Client confidentiality is crucial. Soundproofed rooms, where clients feel safe to share their personal information, is a must.

Excess noise. If there is a lot of noise pollution it could sabotage your clients experience with you and stop them from achieving the full benefit of working with you. This could also stop them from continuing to work with you in the future.

Carpeted floors. Carpets would not work for someone using lots of creams or oils where there could be spillages, as floors need to be easy to clean.

Home practice

Working from home is a great option to save you money on rent, which can take up a large chunk of your income. It also saves you travel time and costs.

Before you decide to work from home, you may need permission from your Local Authority, mortgage lender, or landlord, depending on your circumstances and where you live. You will also need to talk to your home insurance company as they may want to review your cover to take into consideration the visitors to your home. Working from home could be subject to different charges such as business rates, and if you are selling your house, capital gains tax.

Working from home means you are inviting strangers into your house. Where possible, have a separate room to work with clients that is easily accessed from the entrance of your home. It means that you can separate your home life from your work life and maintain your own privacy. You will be able to create the right feel for your practice and ensure it is professionally presented.

Ensure there will not be any parking issues for your neighbours, as well as your clients. Your business should not have a detrimental effect on your local community if you want to work harmoniously from home.

Single discipline and multi-discipline clinics

These are a great option for new practitioners, or those moving to a new area. You will be able to establish yourself amongst a client base who is accustomed to paying for complementary health care and be part of a small community of practitioners. In a single discipline clinic, you may be able to provide cover for your colleagues if they are busy or on holiday.

Clinics that have different disciplines are a powerful way to grow your business from cross-referrals. Find a clinic where practitioners work as a team and are encouraged to support each other's businesses. The key to working in these environments is to be able to clearly communicate what you do, and whom you help, with the receptionist and other practitioners (we cover this in Chapter 10, Marketing basics). Make sure you also know what the other practitioners do and whom they work with too.

Some clinics rent rooms by the hour, half-day, or at a daily rate. Usually in this situation, you are responsible for the marketing and administration of your service. You may need to commit to renting specific, regular time blocks in the clinic around the existing practitioners. The downside is paying for the room even if you do not have any clients.

Other clinics are paid a set amount based on the clients you see, often around 40 per cent of the fee you charge. This generally covers your room rent, reception services, marketing and administration such as taking payments. While this appears expensive, you only pay for the clients you see and you know exactly what you earn per client.

Rented rooms

As well as renting rooms in clinics, you can also consider serviced offices, hotels and other complementary businesses such as health food stores, coffee shops, or hairdressers. Be creative in where you find suitable rooms, ensure they comply with your professional body requirements, and always keep your client at the heart of the decision.

When I started out as a practitioner offering hypnotherapy and coaching sessions, I rented rooms from my local osteopath and a hairdresser with private beauty rooms. This worked brilliantly because I had suitable rooms and as both were busy places where the clients chatted a lot, I got referrals too.

Online services

Technology gives you the opportunity to grow your business and promote your services to a much wider audience, extending beyond your local area. There are huge cost savings available and you get to work from home with the potential for reaching large, international audiences. The disadvantages are isolation, security, and missing the personal connection you get when you are in the same room as someone.

Your code of conduct will outline what is acceptable for your discipline, check with your professional body before deciding if this is an option for you.

If you are selecting a communication platform, ensure it conforms to the regulations in your country and provides a secure online video system for your clients. As a side note, make sure you are also covered to work online by your insurance.

Practitioner safety

By its very nature, the work you do with your clients is personal. Occasionally, what is a kind gesture or comment from you, could get misconstrued and potentially lead to complications. The vast majority of clients you work with will be respectful of the therapeutic relationship. There is however, a very slim chance someone may not be. I do not want to frighten you, but you need to be aware of ways to maximise your safety to protect yourself, especially if you are working alone.

If you work from somewhere other than your home, use your practice address on all correspondence and marketing. If this is not an option you could use a PO Box number which you can get easily from the Post Office (in the UK). This way your home address is kept private and will provide you with a layer of anonymity.

Working from home. Try and separate your working area from the rest of your house. This will help you to separate your life from work, but also keep your personal living space private.

If you intend working from home on a regular basis, you could consider getting an alarm. There are a number of options available, contact your local crime prevention officer or security specialist for guidance.

Working alone. If you work on your own or are doing house calls, make sure you tell someone you have clients, and let them know when you are done. If you are out on a call, it is a great idea to put a tracker on your phone so someone can access your location if necessary. Keep a personal alarm close, even if no-one is in earshot it will be a great deterrent to someone not behaving appropriately.

When working in any room, always position yourself nearest to the door and never put your client between you and the door. This will stop you from being blocked from exiting the room if you wish to.

Have a "need assistance" strategy so you can inform someone if you feel you need help. This can be done by phone with a code word or sentence which raises the alarm. My husband worked as an estate agent for many years and used this technique with his colleagues who were regularly out at different houses. They would call the office with a "please can you pick the dog up from the vets". Something which sounds normal or reasonable to the person listening in, but to their colleagues they would know something was wrong.

If you are working from an office building or similar, if possible only see clients when there are others around. If you do not have a choice about this, make sure you follow the advice of checking in with someone and keep your safety a priority.

If you feel unsure or unhappy with someone or a situation, trust your instinct, it is trying to tell you something. You have the right to say no to working with someone or to end a session if you feel that there is a potential problem. All new clients are strangers until you get to know them and build a professional relationship with them. Start your relationship by setting clear boundaries, so they know what is or is not acceptable. This will help you to maintain a professional relationship and avoid any grey areas in the long term.

Knowing you have taken steps to keep yourself safe will help you to relax with your clients and be able to do your best work.

Understanding your finances

It may sound boring, but knowing your numbers is key to a thriving practice. In order to provide the best service to your clients you need to feel valued and secure in your work. Part of that comes from having enough money coming in to pay your bills and afford the things you want.

It is important that you understand your finances, even if it is in the simplest terms. This way you will know what you need to earn, and from that, work out what you are going to do to achieve it.

I am not an accountant, but I am organised when it comes to my finances. Growing up my dad used to say, "a good accountant will save you far more than they cost". I now realise a good accountant is something I cannot afford to be without. They will help you to work efficiently within the maze of financial regulations, whilst making you the most from your hard-earned income. They will also advise you on the best business structures and make sure you are aware of your legal financial obligations.

Your cost of living

It is important to understand how much you need to earn each month to cover your cost of living. The reality for many practitioners is that they have other jobs which subsidise their practice while they build it, which can take years. You need to know how much you need to earn, so you can ensure you have different income streams in place, if necessary.

EXERCISE: Your cost of living

Realistically list all your monthly outgoings and make sure you include an allowance for the things you pay for every six or 12 months such as car tax or holidays. This shows you how much money you need each month, to maintain your lifestyle. It will help you decide when you need to subsidise your income and when your business is able to support you.

Business money

There are basic numbers you need to track, to understand how well your business is running and what money you have available.

Income. It is important to know what income is coming into your business and where it is coming from in terms of your clients and services. Tracking these will allow you to identify the things that are working for you and those that are not.

Payments. As well as knowing which clients are buying what, you need to know that you have actually been paid. This way you can quickly chase any late payers.

Expenses. This shows where you spend money to provide your services and products. It will also show you places you are spending money you may be able to cut back on.

Fixed costs or overheads. These are the things you have to pay for each month, regardless of whether you see clients or not, for example professional fees, staff, equipment, and insurance.

Cost of sales. These are the costs associated with seeing clients or providing products. They could include room rent, remedies, and credit card transaction fees.

Simple accounts

If you are a sole trader and you do not see a huge number of clients you can start by managing your accounts on a spreadsheet. Set up a simple spreadsheet for each year, with separate pages for income and expenditure and one that provides a summary combining your income and expenditure. Include a column on your income sheet to note when you have been paid. This will clearly show if anyone owes you money which you can then act on.

If you are growing and have lots of different income streams to your business it is best to upgrade to accounting software. There are many online options available that will allow you to do your accounts from your phone as well as allowing access to those who support you. Before purchasing any software, speak with your accountant first. They understand your accounts and will be a great source of support, especially in the early days of setting up your system.

However, to prepare your accounts you need to make sure you keep all receipts relating to business expenses. If you get into this habit you will save yourself money because nothing will be missing. A simple folder in your desk drawer where you put all receipts works perfectly, and once you have accounted for them you file them away.

Schedule time in your diary every month to do your accounts. If you are organised, it will only take a couple of hours. You will know exactly where you are in your business and it will help you decide your next steps.

Keeping a close track on our accounts allows you to make informed and timely decisions about your business. If you do not have enough money coming in you need to take action, and identifying this early on in the process can be the difference between creating a successful and sustainable practice, and failing. It is only when you are in full control of your finances that you will know what money you have available to invest in new equipment and training to allow you and your practice to thrive.

Another advantage of staying on top of your accounts is to avoid finding yourself in the horrible position of trying to piece together your accounts at the end of the year, trying to remember what you did and when and trying to find missing receipts. Staying organised will make for a stress-free tax return and avoid the risk of an unexpected tax bill.

Building in buffers

We live in an unpredictable world and there are often unforeseen circumstances that can catch us off guard. We do not know if the trains will be on time, whether a client will miss an appointment, or if we will catch a virus. The only thing we can expect is the unexpected!

Our options are to either react to the situation by firefighting or doing some preparation in advance, by building in a buffer. A good buffer will lessen or shield you from the impact of something. A buffer will not be the answer to every challenge you face, but it will certainly make life easier.

How often do you find yourself in situations where you are late, or you do not have time for a project, or have no money and no clients booked in? These times massively increase our stress levels and stop us from being resilient and performing at our best. For some reason, most people are optimists when it comes to travelling, often underestimating just how long it takes to get to a place. They only allow for the actual travelling but not for de-icing the car or parking it!

By consistently building in a buffer, the times that were once challenging will become simpler and less stressful. It will not be long before you are feeling much more organised, in control, and calmer. We can never fully anticipate or plan for what will happen, life is just too unpredictable. Buffers will provide you with a little wiggle room and reduce the stress caused by unforeseen circumstances.

EXERCISE: Building in buffers

Identify situations where you would benefit from having buffers in place. Note down the times when you get stressed and overwhelmed, or where you spend your time worrying or feeling guilty. These could be ideal situations to take the pressure off yourself with buffers.

Pick one or two of the areas you have just identified, do not try to do everything in one go. Think about how you can build in a buffer to help you get through the situation. The main solution is to get organised in advance, it will save you time and stress in the process.

A few ideas are:

- Batch cook food so that you have your meals ready for the week
- Sort out your clothes the evening before so you know exactly what you are going to wear
- Get a part-time job to help support you while you build your practice
- Add in extra time to each journey to allow for any delays

Write down the buffers you commit to creating in your life and business.

TAKEAWAY

Putting the right foundations in place and being organised from the start of your business will pay dividends later.

CASE STUDY

Name: Lola Phillips

Discipline: Osteopath and Sports Therapist

Website: healthinmotion.org.uk/

Lola works full-time in her business and founded her welcoming, contemporary clinic where she employs other osteopaths and support staff. She offers a range of services to her local community and has been far more successful than she thought she could be. Lola had to employ other practitioners quickly to meet demand.

Why did you decide to become a practitioner?

Working as an accountant for a pharmaceutical company, I got to understand about disease, epidemiology and drugs. At that time, I thought to myself, if I was starting again, I would have done medical training. I enjoyed my work in the corporate world but did not find it satisfying. This caused me frustration and lack of purpose so I took some time out, did some travelling and was inspired to re-train as an osteopath—I wanted to find something useful to do.

What is your vision for your business?

I knew I wanted to be well known and established within a community and be the go-to person regarding health and healing. I also wanted to employ other osteopaths to provide them with security rather than be self-employed which is how most work.

What are the most important things to date that have helped you grow your business?

1. From my own mixed experience with different healthcare providers (both private and NHS), I knew exactly what I wanted my clients to experience under my care. I reflect these values in my own practice ensuring my clinic and practitioners are organised, caring, focused on the client's problem and have a plan for getting them sorted.

2. All my marketing embodies what I stand for and hopefully expresses my desire to create a therapeutic relationship with clients, rather than merely selling treatments. This approach has enabled the clinic to successfully build relationships within my community. People find me through word of mouth referrals and from my website, which I had professionally designed. I have never done any paid advertising.

I am involved in my local community and participate in events such as the annual summer and Christmas fairs where we run games for the children and hand out goodie bags.

3. The location of the clinic is important as the area is family orientated and we get multiple generations of families coming to us. It is a good place for building a relationship-based practice. I also had a professional designer create the look and layout of my clinic to help it stand out in the local area and attract attention. This was important as there is another Osteopathy clinic located four doors from my new premises. We needed a contemporary look that would generate curiosity and conversations.

With hindsight, is there anything you would have done differently?

I would follow my convictions sooner. It was seven years after I qualified before I got my premises, I wish I had done it sooner. Although it does take time to develop and build as a practitioner so maybe it was good to wait.

The area that has been most challenging is finding staff and other therapists that are on the same page as me. I have a winning formula with patients but finding the right colleagues and getting the right chemistry and understanding is still work in progress as extending your values is difficult.

What is next for your business?

I want to do more within the profession running small courses and networking opportunities from my clinic. I am interested in teaching the softer skills that you do not learn at osteopathy school.

CHAPTER SIX

Creating Your Personal Brand

Practitioners often think of a brand in terms of a logo and a few chosen colours, but it is so much more. How your clients experience your services, your location, your voice, and how you communicate will all reflect on you and help people to form an opinion about your brand. Your brand and the values it stands for are based on everything communicated by you and your business, even down to individual relationships. It is how you make people feel and how you are perceived which creates a set of expectations.

People will judge your brand on everything they see and experience, so you need consistency throughout your business and your marketing.

You are your brand

When it comes to personal branding and marketing yourself as a practitioner, there is no better way to build relationships and stand out than to be yourself. It is much easier than trying to be someone you are not.

Placing yourself at the heart of your business, you start with your "why". You did the work on this in Chapter 4, Creating your dream practice. Knowing what you stand for, what you believe in, and your cause will help you to define your brand and find your voice.

Your messages and marketing activities will be genuine and reflect you as an individual. It will be much easier for you to reach out to people and connect with them. People buy from people, especially in health and well-being. Rapport is crucial to a trusting relationship and your clients will want to get to know the real you.

Authentic marketing

Authentic marketing starts with embracing who you are as a unique individual. It is sharing the different facets of your personality, experience, knowledge, opinions, qualities, and stories that build a relationship with your audience. It is about being bold, standing up, and being visible despite your fears. It is about being a real person talking to other real people, sharing and having conversations.

As a practitioner, a certificate may prove a qualification, but the therapeutic relationship requires a far deeper connection. We have an idea of what it is to be the "perfect practitioner" and put pressure on ourselves to be that person. If you present yourself as whom you think you should be instead of who you are there will be a disconnect and it will be hard work to maintain. It is not unusual to see practitioners marketing themselves in the same way as their peers, thinking that is what they should do too. This copycat marketing stops you from standing out and will not be a good reflection of you, or your brand.

Before you even start working with clients, they will want to understand what makes you tick. This is where authentic marketing is the key to helping you build a connection and trust with potential clients. This marketing will also reinforce your relationship with existing clients and reinforce why they chose you in the first place.

We grow up often thinking different is bad or undesirable. It is your unique characteristics that make you attractive to the right people and it is these clients who will get the best results from working with you.

Be bold, stand up, and say "this is who I am, and this is what I stand for". It can be scary and you will encounter people who do not like it, that is fine as they are not the right clients for you anyway. You want to repel the people who are not a good fit because they will not get the results and will sap your energy in the process.

It is time to take off the mask and start to own who you really are, including the bits that scare you. The quirks that make you unique will help you stand out and connect with others.

EXERCISE: Marketing yourself authentically

Determine exactly what and how much to share by deciding your personal boundaries and sticking to them. Just because you share generously, it does not mean you have to hang out your dirty laundry for everyone to see! Be sensitive to family and friends who may not want to participate in your marketing activities.

You do not have to do everything at once, start by taking small steps when deciding what to share. Identify something you are willing to share about yourself and start there. Be consistent, sharing similar things and as you get more comfortable add something else to the mix.

Write in your notebook the things you are happy to share and the things you are keeping private as a reminder.

SABOTEUR ALERT: Being visible

When you step out of your comfort zone and allow yourself to be visible it will throw up any self-limiting beliefs you have about yourself. These beliefs can keep us hidden and playing small to avoid anything that scares you.

Start to notice the beliefs you have which are getting in the way of you being a successful practitioner, they will often be hiding in the stories you tell yourself. What is stopping you from being visible? Write them down in your notebook and look at them objectively. Is allowing these beliefs to continue useful to your business? If they are sabotaging you they need to be addressed to allow you to flourish.

Decide what you want to believe instead and write the new beliefs down. Now use your favoured method to work on creating the new, more useful, beliefs. If you feel really stuck, work with your chosen practitioner or coach to address this and help develop new beliefs that will support your success.

Building connections with your story

Story is an incredibly powerful way to communicate. It has been used throughout history to pass information from generation to generation. Stories help people to understand complex ideas and remember events.

A story is a brilliant way to breathe life into your marketing and connect to the people you want to help.

When I first worked as a practitioner, I missed this point completely! My biography was very factual describing how I changed career because I wanted to make a difference blah, blah, blah. Whilst this was true, there was nothing that connected me to the reader on an emotional level. It was what I thought people wanted to hear, but I was very wrong. I realised I was hiding so I started to tell my story, of why I originally trained as a practitioner. I allowed myself to be vulnerable and shared how I had dealt with my personal demons of perfection and low self-esteem. It was scary to admit my faults as I saw them, but this was a huge turning point for me. I started to get clients wanting to work with me because they had connected with my story.

Start to think about the qualities which attract people to you. What common themes run through your story? What are you always being asked to help with?

When looking for help, people do not just want to read theory, they want to connect. Your story will help them to understand and trust who you are as a person and as a practitioner. When you connect to your audience with your story, people will get it.

Once you start sharing your story, identify which aspects resonate with your favourite clients. Take these elements and weave them into your marketing. There will be longer and shorter versions, but they will all share a common theme.

Your marketing will get easier, and once you are comfortable with your story and your qualities you start to peel away the mask. You will not be constantly second-guessing what you should say, you simply answer as you.

EXERCISE: Your story

Grab your notebook and spend a few minutes free writing your story without thinking about it. You can refine it later but start by getting it out of your head in an unedited way. Once you have it all down, write the first draft and return to it regularly to review and tailor it until you have something that flows. It is worth asking a trusted friend to review it and provide you with some objective feedback on your story.

Your story will continuously evolve and that is okay. We are all a "work in progress" and moving in different seasons of our life and business.

RECOMMENDED READING: *How the World Sees You* **by Sally Hogshead**

This is a great book to learn how to succinctly communicate your qualities by discovering how others see you and the true value you provide them. The aim is to unlearn being boring where you have camouflaged yourself to blend in and instead learn how to stand out using the science and art of fascination.

The steps will help you recognise what makes you different and identify a few words (your anthem) to describe yourself and your personality. These can be used on your social media profiles and be woven into your marketing messages. Being able to communicate with this clarity will help you attract the right clients and repel those who are not a good fit.

When I read it, I knew exactly where I fell within the archetypes and every ounce of me was rebelling against it. I had spent many years feeling I was boring because I was so sensible. Reading this book helped me to recognise that being pragmatic and level-headed is what attracts my clients to me! It helped me to embrace my inner "Captain Sensible" (my husband's nickname for me) which has made marketing myself so much easier.

Creating your brand

We have already established you are your brand, so you need to allow your personality to shine through. If you already have a brand take a close look at it and think about the following:

- Do I love this brand?
- Does it reflect me and my values?
- What does it communicate?

Before you start creating or updating your brand, consider the following questions and note down your answers in your notebook. They will help you to brief a designer if you are using one to create your logo and brand style.

Why do I do what I do? This is about getting into the emotions of why you do what you do and creating your story, it is your passion and what drives your work. Refer to the work you did in Chapter 4, Creating your dream practice.

What values do I want my brand to reflect? These are the things you stand for in your business and what you want to be known for.

What do I do? This needs to have an emotional attachment to the answer which makes a person want to dig deeper and ask more questions. Just making the statement, I am a counsellor or an osteopath does not set you apart from all the others in your field, you need to expand upon this to include areas of specialism and what is unique about your approach.

How do I do what I do? Think about all the things you do to provide your services or products. Chose the top three points that demonstrate this.

Who is my ideal client? By understanding who your ideal client is you will be able to create a brand and message to speak directly to them. This is important to make sure your marketing is effective and appeals to the right people rather than trying to appeal to everyone and missing out completely. We will cover this in Chapter 17, Your clients.

How do I want to be perceived? Think about the aspects of your personality you want to reflect within your business. Create a personality for your brand and write down the different characteristics it would have if it was a person.

Positioning yourself

In its simplest terms, positioning is how your brand sits in the mind of your favourite client and determines how you connect with them. It decides where you appear in relation to your competition and how you distinguish yourself from them.

How you position yourself can be responsible for how you build your brand and the strategies you choose to connect with prospective clients. It will determine your services and how they are packaged, how much you charge, and ultimately will affect how successful your business will be.

Being able to clearly articulate whom you help, and whom you do not help will assist you in positioning yourself. You want to create a situation where you attract people who will benefit from working with you and repel those who are not a good fit. Your position lets people know what to expect from you and whether you are the right person for them to work with.

Your positioning is integral to your branding and represented in everything you do in your business. Patience is a virtue. Brands and positioning take time to establish, they do not happen overnight. Having the courage to take a stance on your position will help you to build a sustainable, thriving practice.

EXERCISE: Talking points

Once you understand your brand and what it stands for, think about the topics you want to be known for. These can include both professional and personal talking points and hobbies. Make a list in your notebook of the main topics to help keep your marketing activities and social media posts relevant. Then pass everything you post through that filter to make sure it aligns with the topics you want to be known for.

Logo and style

You are now able to start work on the look of your brand. Having a well-designed, consistent brand will help you build your profile, reflect your values and stand out in your chosen field. If possible, hire a graphic designer to create your logo and style for you. They will be able to take your brief and translate it into something that represents you brilliantly, looks professional and will work in different situations.

DIY logo

If you do not have the budget to employ a graphic designer you can create your own logo and once you are established it can be re-visited if necessary. Avoid using anything like clipart as it will tend to make your logo look cheap and homemade and you may have copyright issues using someone else's artwork.

Keep it simple and pick a font (typeface) that you already have on your computer, one that you like and is easy to read. Choose a colour you like and one you think your clients will respond well to. If you want inspiration on what colours to pick look up the psychology of colour. There are some great articles online telling you the meaning behind different colours. Now create your logo using your font and colour and make a note of them. This is your simple logo to use in all of your marketing.

Create your colour palette

Once you have picked your main colour pick one or two colours that complement or contrast with it. Having different colours will help your marketing look more interesting and you can weave them into your graphics which will give your brand consistency. For example, my main colour is teal but I also use gold and coral, which appear throughout my marketing.

Create your brand guidelines

This is simply a reference page that includes your logo, colours, and any other aspects relating to your brand such as specifying fonts for your copy. This is your go-to reference point for any marketing or communication materials you create for your business, whether it is your website, a presentation, workbooks, or client information.

Once you have your logo and colour, decide on a font that complements your logo which you will use for all your text. You can have a second font for headings to give some extra interest but ensure you limit the number of fonts you use, or things will start to look messy. Keeping to one or two fonts will help everything you produce have a common look and feel about it.

Brand guidelines are a really useful document to give to anyone working with you such as a graphic designer or virtual assistant as it will help them keep your branding consistent. Include the following information:

- Logo
- Colours (include the colour references)
- Headings font and size
- Text font and size
- Talking points and topics

Profile photo

You are your business, so your profile photo plays a huge role in your branding. Your photo should reflect the image you want to portray in your business. It is not good enough to use a photo from a party or holiday for your website or social media profiles. Your photograph is about connecting you with people and clients, so you want them to be a professional reflection of you.

Investing in professional photography is a great investment for your brand and should be a priority once you have the budget. A photographer will know how to set up the shots and how to get the best results for you and they will also be able to advise you on what will work to fit with your branding.

Profile shots should also be updated regularly and especially if you make any big changes to your appearance. Scarily we all get older too and you do not want someone having a shock when they meet you because you look nothing like you do in your photo.

Taking time to think about your photos in advance of taking them will be well worth the effort. Ask yourself these questions:

What do I need photographs for? By knowing where you are likely to use your photos, you can plan how to take them. This will make life easy for yourself when you come to use them, for example, images for websites are usually landscape and need a lot of background. By leaving space around you in the photos you can add text over the background.

What will I wear? Does your outfit suit your discipline and business? Does it match your brand colours? Do you feel comfortable and happy? Pick a few outfits so you have different options to choose from.

Where can I be photographed? If you do not have access to professional lighting, it is best to take photos in natural daylight but not in full sunlight.

What is in the background? Remember this will show up in your photos so what looks right? If you are intending on putting text over the background, will that work?

If you do not have the resources to hire a professional team up with a friend who takes a good photo to create your profile shots. Take lots of different photos, as you can delete any you do not like. It is better to have more to pick from, than not enough. Relax and have fun, the more relaxed you are the better you will capture photos which reflect you and your brand.

TAKEAWAY

Your personal brand is not just your logo, it is how you are perceived and how you make people feel. The more consistent you can be with your messages and marketing, the more professional you will appear.

CHAPTER SEVEN

Your Clients

To be happy in your business, it is important you enjoy working with your clients and helping them with their problems. New practitioners often start out working as generalists while they find their niche. Many established practitioners continue to stay working as generalists as they fear they will be limiting their opportunities by picking a niche. Ultimately, it is your business and your decision whom you work with, but if you are struggling I urge you to review your choice.

What is a generalist?

A generalist offers their services to anyone who can benefit without identifying themselves as a specialist in a specific area. In the medical world, you would be a general practitioner (GP), working with the general public, presenting with any issue, rather than a consultant specialising in a particular field. There are advantages to being a generalist:

- You will have a broader set of skills across a range of different issues
- It will help you understand other problems your clients may present with

- You will be able to see the bigger picture
- There is more scope to learn about different things

However, from a marketing perspective there are many disadvantages to being a generalist. Whilst having the potential to work with anyone may feel like an obvious choice, unfortunately the reality is very different. Offering to help everyone will make your marketing invisible and you will not stand out amongst the plethora of other practitioners and disciplines. It will be difficult to articulate the benefits to your prospective clients of why they should work with you instead of a specialist. Unless your discipline is well known and understood by the general public, you may struggle to survive as a generalist.

It will be hard to build your authority as a generalist and this can lead to lost opportunities, such as speaking at conferences. People are willing to pay premium prices for specialists so as a generalist, it may be difficult to charge what you are worth.

There is a space between being a generalist and specialising and this is where the magic happens. This is where you are an expert in a niche, but you can help your clients with other things if the opportunity arises. Generalists often fear picking a niche because they are scared of missing out on potential clients. Instead, they try to market themselves as all things to all people but end up with empty diaries. If you are a generalist and you are struggling to find clients, I recommend you pick a niche.

Choosing a niche

When I use the term niche, I am referring to those people who are your favourite clients. The ones you want to help and get the best results for. They are the people you write your marketing message for, to let them know you can help. Having a niche does not stop you from working with everyone, it just focuses your marketing activities. It helps you to become known for helping people in specific ways.

Having a niche is particularly important if you include online marketing activities in your chosen strategies or want to create income from online activities. When someone is searching for help with their problems online, they will not use or type generic questions in the search engines, they will be specific with what they ask for.

What is a niche? A niche is a well-defined group of people whom you offer your products and services to. They will have things in common such as their challenges, problems, and issues and will share similar lifestyles, interests, and backgrounds. Importantly, they are the kind of clients that you want to work with, and you can help.

What a niche is not. Just because you pick a niche it does not stop you from working with other clients if the opportunity arises. Successfully working with clients can lead to recommendations which may be outside of your niche. It does not mean you cannot see these clients and a niche does not have to be your whole business.

Picking a niche is not a forever decision, you can change it at a later date if it is not a good fit or not working out the way you want.

Why niche? The benefit of selecting a niche is it focuses your marketing efforts. It makes it very clear whom you are communicating to, and you can tailor your messages effectively. Having a well-defined niche makes it simple for people to understand exactly who you work with, even if it is not them personally they can relay your message to a friend or family member who does need your help.

Picking a niche is likely to bring you faster results from your marketing as people are actively sourcing help for their specific problems. People are naturally sceptical and especially so when it comes to their health and well-being. They want to know they are consulting an expert who is experienced in helping people just like them.

When you are viewed as an expert within a certain field you are more likely to be presented with other opportunities such as being asked for your opinion by the press, invited to speak on the topic, or write a book.

EXERCISE: Finding your niche

Grab your notebook and ask yourself the following questions to help you choose your niche:

- Who are your current clients?
- Who are you excited about working with?
- What specific problems do you solve?
- Who will pay for your solutions?
- Which group of people do you have the most contacts for and access to?
- What issues are you experienced in working with?
- Which group of clients feels the most natural for you to work with?
- Is this group large enough to provide you with regular clients?

If you are a new practitioner, think about the people you have access to in your personal network and those you practised with during your training for ideas.

Now make a decision on your niche:

- Which is the easiest group for you to work with at this time?
- Where are you most likely to find clients and feel confident helping them achieve results?

Six-month commitment

Marketing is a marathon not a sprint and it will take time to establish your niche. Once you have chosen it commit to marketing consistently to this group for at least the next six months. This will give it the chance to build momentum and help you to understand if it is viable. At the end of the six months, you can review where you are with your niche and decide if you want to continue to grow it keep it and expand into another area with a second niche, or if it is not working change to a different one.

Understanding your clients

One of the easiest ways to ensure your marketing connects with people is by listening to what your clients have to say. If you are new, find people who represent your chosen niche and speak to them. By really understanding how they feel, their dreams, hopes, struggles, and fears, you can tailor your marketing to show how you can help them, in a way that resonates with them.

Language is an incredibly powerful tool and can make or break your marketing efforts. It is the architecture of how we think, express ourselves, and communicate. By tapping into the specific words and phrases your clients use you can communicate with them personally. If you help people with performance anxiety, would someone who feels sick when they are about to give a presentation realise you can help them? Not necessarily! Instead, if you ask: "do you feel sick when you stand up to give a presentation?", they absolutely know you get them. This is the type of information you will gain from taking time to research and understand your clients.

Not everyone will use the exact same phrases, but you will see common threads if you speak with enough people. You can then start weaving these phrases into your marketing. Knowing how your favourite clients describe where they feel stuck and what they need help with is priceless. It will allow you to use their words to attract more clients, just like them.

The simplest and most effective way to do this is through conversation. Speaking with people allows you to dig deeper into a topic and find out information that may not be shared in a questionnaire.

Contact your current clients (or people who represent your ideal client group) and ask if they are willing to spare you 15 minutes for a chat as you are doing some research into their needs. The more calls with different people you can do the better, as they will help you really get to the heart of how your clients feel. This call is about listening, understanding their issues and, especially, the emotions behind them. You can ask further questions to gain a deeper understanding of what is really going on for them. This exercise is about discovering the precise language clients use and not about trying to coach or fix them.

Create a simple template for yourself and fill it in during the conversation, writing down their answers word for word. This will help to keep you on track and focus on asking the questions you want answered. I have included examples of questions you can ask in the exercise below, keep it to three of four key questions so you have time to discuss each one. To get a deeper understanding, you can ask the person to clarify how it makes them feel or to tell you more about it.

EXERCISE: Making research calls

Start with a warm welcome and set the scene for the call.

Follow this up with a few specific questions to help you to understand your client's needs better and the problems you can help them resolve. For example:

- *"What are your biggest challenges with (your topic)?"*
  This will help you to understand exactly how your client describes the problem they have and how it affects them.
- *"If you could fix these challenges (list the challenges you identified in response to the first question) how different would life be?"*
  This will give you an insight into the benefits they will get from resolving their issues and how it will feel emotionally.

- *"What have you already tried to fix them?"*
  This will help you understand the approaches they have tried so far. This will let you know if they have invested time and money into resolving the issue so far. It will allow you to see where your services or products fit as a potential solution for your clients.
- *"What would your ideal solution be?"*
  Use this question to understand exactly what people are looking for and how they want it provided. This will help you deliver your products and services in a way your clients want and provide ideas for developing future offerings.

Finish on time with a big *"Thank you!"* and ask if they would like to hear more about your solutions when they are available. Keep a list of anyone saying yes so you can contact them when you are ready.

When you have finished all your calls, go through the answers and highlight phrases that come up over and over again. These are the exact words you want to incorporate into your marketing and help potential clients understand exactly how you can help them.

You can download a template for these research calls at helenharding. co.uk/bonus.

Online research

Whilst talking to clients is absolutely the best way of getting a deep understanding of their problems and issues, some very useful information can also be gained online.

Online survey software. There are lots of great free survey software available which you can use to create surveys with open-ended or multiple-choice questions. Before choosing one, make sure it is compliant with data regulations in your country. Once set up, you have a link which you can email or share on social media to collect answers. When the survey is finished, simply download the information to analyse the responses.

Online surveys are great, but they do take effort to complete. Some people are put off responding as they think it will take a long time. Keep them short and make sure people know they are only three questions long or will take two minutes to complete.

Online groups and forums. These are a great place to learn about your niche. Research groups and forums where your ideal clients hang out and look at the conversations they have there and the questions they ask. You will get a good idea of the challenges they face and how they feel about them.

TAKEAWAY

Picking a niche will laser focus your marketing and allow you to tailor your messages directly to your favourite client in a way they understand.

CASE STUDY

Name: Ellen Waldren
Discipline: Counsellor and Therapist
Website: counselling-directory.org.uk/counsellors/ellen-waldren
Ellen works three days a week with clients giving her long weekends to herself. The work Ellen is really interested in is the more challenging mental health issues like Obsessive-Compulsive Disorder where issues are entrenched. She is very clear labelling it as a "disorder" is not helpful! Ellen wants to inspire her clients to find hope, it is not an impossible task, it can be done with work.

Why did you decide to become a practitioner?

I worked as a head-hunter and recruiter in the city for many years. I was successful, but I felt jaded and started to feel my age. I wanted to find something else that had longevity and utilised the skills I had built up over the 30 years of recruiting. Knowing how to develop relationships and understanding people's needs dovetailed nicely into training as a counsellor.

What is your vision for your business?

I am in the lucky situation where it is not about the money, it is something else that drives me. I want to create something that feels fulfilling for me as much as it does my clients and is something I enjoy. I am naturally curious, and I see myself as a detective where I help to put the jigsaw together. I help people build more compassion towards themselves, we are hugely hard on ourselves

What are the most important things to date that have helped you grow your business?

1. Building self-belief, knowing I am not an imposter and I can do this effectively was my biggest realisation in terms of my own growth and personal development. I became more effective as I really started to believe in myself and became less critical. I was much more congruent working with my clients, and I became more confident talking about what I do and started to promote myself in a way that did not feel sleazy.
2. My location and being able to work from home are really important, as I did not want to have to go to work. I have the perfect space which is completely separate from my home and lends itself to a lovely experience for both me and my clients.
3. Embracing new ideas that are not so much controversial but outside of my own experience and opening myself up to other approaches that would have seemed like snake oil a few years ago. The fact that your mental health impacts physical health, and vice versa, which has become more and more apparent.

With hindsight, is there anything you would have done differently?

I would have specialised earlier and niched down. When I started, I wanted to be all things to all people. If I could give myself one piece of advice, it would be to specialise sooner and know it is better to specialise and dominate one niche to become the go-to person.

I would not be afraid to change tack. Just because you invest so much time, effort and money, it can feel like you cannot get off the runaway train, but I believe you can. Do not be afraid to change, as scary as that sounds, especially if you have done something for a long time and you have always done it like that. It is called "familiar pain"!

What is next for your business?

Things are going alright at the moment and I do not need more clients, but I want to be more effective, so I have been doing more training to improve my tool kit. I want to give clients some relief quickly and move them towards a twelve-week programme rather than an ongoing model where they are with me for the long term. It is much more business-like and purposeful. If clients get some fast changes with the immediate things that are troubling them now, they will build their confidence, and then they can work on the deeper stuff.

CHAPTER EIGHT

Your Services and Products

Ultimately, whatever you sell, whether it is products or services, you are selling an experience. It is the experience a client has as a result of working with you and how they felt which will be remembered, and your products and services play a big role in this.

The starting point for most practitioners is to offer one-to-one sessions, selling one at a time to each client. This is a good way to get your business up and running and build your experience and confidence. The downside is having repeat conversations about booking the next session. Delaying appointments or not getting around to re-booking could cost clients their results, and lose you business.

When you work in person on a one-to-one basis, you are swapping time for money and there will be a ceiling to what you can earn. If this suits you, brilliant! But you could consider packaging your services to provide more stability for your practice.

When offering packages and products be mindful of your professional body's code of conduct, there may be limitations about what you can offer within your discipline.

Packaging your services and products

Packaging is grouping together sessions and other elements, if you have them, to provide your clients with great value. Well thought out packages will help you to stand out from the competition. By including extras that do not require you to fulfil them personally you will add value and provide extra support without tying up more of your time. There is also the opportunity to sell any products you design separately and create other income streams for your practice.

Packages and products provide your clients with options. You may find having a lower-priced offering allows people to experience your approach before making bigger investments. Keep it simple especially with the number of packages you offer, or it could have the opposite effect and overwhelm potential clients.

When you start looking to create packages, consider the logistics of working with your clients. When working on the main issues you solve for your clients, look at the following:

- How many sessions do they normally need and how often?
- Are they one-to-one or can they be in groups?
- Do you need to see them in person, or can you work remotely?
- Do you focus on providing a specific result or ongoing support?

Research your options to see what else is out there. What other packages and products do your clients buy? Look at those that are similar to what you offer, and those that are different, as these could provide you with inspiration. Knowing the type of packages people buy will allow you to tailor your offering, giving yourself the best chance of success. Also, speak to your clients and find out what support they would like from you and what else you could provide that would be useful for them.

Digital products

These can be offered in addition to your sessions or packages or as stand-alone products. They will help your clients get the most value from your services. Where possible, have products that, once created, are provided without a lot of additional work from you. A few ideas include:

- Herbalists—seasonal foraging guides and recipes for homemade remedies

- Hypnotherapists—guided hypnosis download and a guide to creating a great morning routine
- Nutritionists—meal planners, recipes, and a kitchen cupboard essentials shopping list
- Yoga teachers—videos for mini-workouts, five-minute guided meditations, and printouts of affirmations

Technology provides a huge opportunity to deliver DIY programmes to clients and provide an additional income stream to your business. Is there something you could create for your clients so they can help themselves? There are all sorts of digital products you can create and sell such as books, online course, workbooks, audio downloads, diaries, or cheat sheets. Once created, you will have to market the products, but they should take very little of your time to deliver once the initial work has been done to create them. These products could also form the basis of a workshop you run or be created into physical products to sell such as journals or diaries.

RECOMMENDED READING: *Wellpreneur* by Amanda Cooke

If you want to create digital products as an additional income stream for your business and learn how to market yourself online this book is written specifically for complementary practitioners. Amanda walks you through her "Organic Growth System" to set up your health and well-being business online. You will be able to use a lot of the work you are doing in this book to feed into her system and start building your online presence.

Create your packages

Considering your business, what type of packages would work best for you and your clients? Here are some ideas for packages:

Packages of sessions. If you usually work with clients for several sessions to achieve great results, look at how you can package them up. To make the packages attractive, offer a discounted rate from your individual sessions. If you offer six sessions for the price of five your client will have an incentive to buy the package and commit to doing the work. You will have an inspired client and receive the stability of a guaranteed income to your business. This is the fastest way to add a package to your offerings and can be done with very little work by you. However, ensure you set a realistic time limit for completion of the sessions as you do not want the financial or time implications of honouring a package that was purchased years ago.

Programmes. Creating a programme is a great way to solve a specific problem for your clients. They can be as short as a week or as long as a year. Be aware, people are less likely to commit to something that is too long as it will feel unachievable and like a huge commitment. Work out the best time frame for clients to get great results. You can always add on extra weeks/months if clients require them.

You need to consider how you will deliver your programme, for example, in person, online, or in groups. If you are just starting with programmes, keep it simple and plan it out using the technology you understand and currently have available. Get started and build it up slowly and in a manageable way. Creating a programme is a lot of work. There is always the option of buying a templated system to help you create one quickly.

Group programmes. These are a great way to get clients through your door and experience your approach before committing to a bigger investment. Working in groups can be easier and less time consuming than working individually with clients as they will be following the same structure.

Workshops. These are a great way to share your passion and knowledge. As with the programmes, keep them simple and start small. A medical herbalist could do a herb walk in their local area or a nutritionist could teach classes about healthy eating for busy families. You could also teach your colleagues the skills you have, which they would find helpful professionally.

You will need to be organised but workshops are a great way to introduce clients to your practice in an affordable way.

VIP days. Do you offer a service that can be created into some sort of intensive day or half-day session? This could be with a single person or a small group and is a premium service. It will, however, give your client(s) your full attention for a period of time to address their problems in a really focused way.

Retreats. These are a great way to take your client out of their normal environment and focus on working with them and creating an amazing experience. Retreats are a great opportunity to team up with other practitioners to offer a range of complementary approaches.

How you package your services will change as you start to work out what works and what does not. You will be refining your packages as you go. Before you create anything, check with your professional body for any rules around offering packages.

Minimum viable product

When you start developing any new offering, keep it simple. Start with the minimum viable product (MVP) and create your new product, workshop, or programme with the basic features needed to satisfy your clients.

MVP comes from *The Lean Start-Up* by Eric Ries (2011). The idea is, you start simple and move fast. It will stop you from getting caught up trying to make everything perfect before you launch anything. Waiting for everything to be perfect means you lose sight of the core value you want to provide to your clients and instead get caught up in your own doubts and fears.

However, it must work so take care not to over-simplify. You must meet client expectations as people have minimum standards and it will reflect badly on your brand if they are not met.

Advantages of the MVP approach:

- Produce it quickly as there will be fewer elements to create
- Allows you to test if there is a demand for it before you create the all-singing, all-dancing version
- Avoid large investments of time and money just to find out it does not work
- Gain insights from how your clients use it to identify any improvements needed
- Get new ideas to create other offerings

It is a good idea to beta test your basic workshop, course, or programme and invite people to participate at a reduced price. You let participants know it is the first time you are running it and part of the deal is for them to provide you with feedback. You get the opportunity to make sure it works, is well received, to make any improvements needed, and get testimonials for your marketing.

When you design your offering start with what you have available now. Design it based on the technology, the skills, and the knowledge you already have. If you start thinking you must understand how new fancy technology works before you do it, you will never finish.

Seven steps to creating your MVP

1. **Find your idea.** What are you going to produce to solve a specific problem for your clients?
2. **Outline it.** Keep it as simple as possible. Map out your idea and decide on the basic elements you can produce. Write up an outline of what you want to do.
3. **Validate it.** Offer it to your audience to find out if there is a need for it. Do not take people's word on it being a good idea, get them to sign-up to a waiting list, or better still, pay to participate in the beta test.
4. **Create it.** Take your outline and create the simplest version of your offering. You want to do as good a job as possible with what you have, keeping costs low. You can pay a designer to create a masterpiece once you know it works.
5. **Beta test it.** Run the first version and ask the participants for feedback.
6. **Update and adapt.** Make the changes to your offering and add any flourishes to help it be a full and workable offering.
7. **Sell it.** This is now one of your income-generating offers for clients.

Creating physical products

Creating your own line of physical health and beauty products is a fantastic way of increasing your income but make sure you check out the legal implications first. Regulations vary from country to country and are dependent on the type of product.

You need to ensure any product you produce is professional, well-formulated, and does what it claims to do. They need to be properly safety-tested before you can sell them to the public, which can be expensive depending on the ingredients. Depending on the type of product you are creating, you may have to consider legislation related to:

- Cosmetic Safety
- Product Stability Testing

- Food Standards Agency
- Environmental Health
- Trading Standards

Affiliate marketing

You do not have to provide, produce, or create everything you sell to your clients. You have the opportunity to offer other company's products and services that complement your own. Affiliate marketing is popular with online companies and is big business. In essence, you promote a trusted service or product to your audience, and if they buy it you get a commission from the sale. You will be able to find suitable products and services for your clients to earn extra income.

Being an affiliate is an easy way to add breadth to your product offerings without you having to do everything yourself. You can provide your clients with a fuller service and ensure the products they use are good quality.

Whilst you can offer pretty much anything as an affiliate, do not promote anything you have no experience of, as it could end up harming your reputation. If you have specific products or services you use and love, and you know they will benefit your client, investigate how you can offer them as an affiliate.

Most transactions take place online. A link sends the visitor to an offer and if they buy, you as the affiliate will be paid commission. It is an effective strategy, especially if you have a big online audience.

The companies you work with can be giants where you can promote any product on their website to your clients, or you could find a small micro-business who only have a tiny selection of very specialised products. If you have a company in mind check out their website, details of affiliate schemes can often be found in the footer. If not, contact them to find out if they have a scheme or are willing to discuss one.

If you are promoting physical products as an affiliate you do not have to hold any stock, the company selling is responsible for that. You receive a commission on the sale and do not get involved in any handling of the goods.

For transparency, always make sure people know you are an affiliate for products you are recommending.

Retail

If you have the budget, you could purchase selected products at whole-sale prices and sell them to your clients. This could be in a shop on your website or you could have products on display in your practice. You make your money from the profit of selling the product. This is a good option if you have space, or only have a few items, but you will have to hold and manage the stock and be responsible for delivering it.

TAKEAWAY

Adding packages and products to your offerings are great ways to pro-duce extra income streams to your business and help make it sustainable.

CHAPTER NINE

Setting Your Prices

S etting prices is an emotive topic. You can attract a good flow of clients with amazing marketing, but if you do not have your prices set properly you could still struggle financially.

Pricing acts as a filter. Too expensive and some people are automatically put off, too cheap and your experience and the quality of your services will be questioned. Your pricing is key to the success and sustainability of your business and your lifestyle. No matter what your intentions are in terms of helping people, you must be able to make money to thrive. The following questions will help you to understand what you need to charge in your business:

What do you need to earn to cover your living expenses?

What does your current business look like?

- What is your current business income?
- How many clients do you see?
- What do you earn from different products and services?
- Does your business cover the costs of running it?
- Is there money left over to pay yourself after you have paid your bills?
- How many hours do you work?

What is your capacity? If you imagine your ideal business, what is the maximum number of clients you want to see? Make sure you are being reasonable in terms of how many clients you can work with in any one day.

How do your clients pay you? If someone is paying you from their own pocket they will have a different opinion to someone who is being funded by an insurance company or the NHS.

What do others charge for similar services? This is not to price match them. You will not have the same financial requirements and you are a different person with different experience and skills. This gives you a guide of the different offers available, the experience of the people making the offers and what clients are willing to pay.

What value are you providing your clients? Whilst most people base their pricing on how much they think someone will pay, you should also consider the value you are providing your client. What is working with you worth to them in terms of their life and health? Understanding this and what they have done in the past to resolve the issue will help you pitch your pricing just right. The client research you did in Chapter 7, Your clients will help you figure this out.

Where does each product or service fit within your range? Take a broad view of what you are offering as a total. Identify where each item fits and its value in relation to your other products and services. If you have a workbook, it may be your lowest-priced offering at £10 but you also offer a one-to-one VIP day costing £1,000, with different workshops and clinical sessions in-between. Each item has a different role, each will attract different clients from your niche and needs to work in relation to your other offers.

EXERCISE: Information for setting your prices

Use the numbers you identified in Chapter 3, Reality check, to help you answer the questions above. You may also need to do some additional research. Write your answers in your notebook.

How much should you charge?

There is no one right answer to this question and you will need to test out your pricing to understand what works for you. This is something that can be adjusted but you must start somewhere, and being the cheapest is not usually the best option. Your pricing will communicate your value directly to your prospective clients and will position you in the market as the premier service, the budget range, or somewhere in the middle. Your pricing must reflect the same qualities and values as your brand or there will be a mismatch and it will confuse your clients.

Have a play with your prices. You know what your business costs are, what you need to earn, and how much it costs to see each client. Start to work out how much you charge for your services and what this means to the number of clients you need to work with.

As a rule, the cheaper you are the more clients you get, but this will take up more of your time and energy. Increasing your prices up will change the number of clients you see, but you will earn more money for fewer hours worked.

Working out your pricing

Knowing how many clients you need to see (or how many packages you need to sell) and your business numbers will help you to set realistic prices. Making sure your pricing works for you and your business is the key to you creating a thriving practice. I have walked you through an example using individual client sessions below, you can use a similar formula to work out pricing for your other services and products.

For example (per month):

- Overheads = £500
- Salary = £1,000 (remember to allow for tax etc.)
- Number of clients = 20
- Cost per client = £5 (this is how much it costs you to see each client)

Use this equation to test out your pricing for client appointment fees:

- (Overheads + salary = sum) ÷ number of clients = (sum + cost per client)
- (£500 + £1,000 = £1,500) ÷ 20 (= £75 + £5) = £80 fee (per client appointment)

Get comfortable playing around with the numbers as they will help you identify what works best for you. Try working the figures backwards if you have a set price and want to know if it works financially for you. Using the above figures, if clients were to pay £100 per appointment what salary could you take home?

- (Fee – cost per client) = (sum x number of clients) = (total – overheads) = salary
- (£100 – £5) = (£95 x 20) = (£1,900 – £500) = £1,400 salary

What if you wanted to set your price at a cheaper rate, say £50 per appointment, what would that mean to the number of client appointments you would need to do to still take a salary of £1,000?

- (Overheads + salary = sum) ÷ (fee – cost per client) = number of appointments
- £500 + £1,000 = £1,500 ÷ (£50 – £5 = £45) = 33.3 appointments

These calculations are based on individual client sessions. By having a mix of services and products, you can spread your income across different offerings. This will provide more security to your practice as you will not be dependent on one income stream. If you are not busy in one area of your business, you will be able to subsidise your income with another.

Ultimately, your prices are your decision. Respecting your value does not mean you cannot be flexible for the right reason. If you really want to work with someone and they genuinely cannot afford it, it is your choice. You can decide to offer discounts or be flexible with your service, just make sure you understand how your decision affects your income.

Setting budgets

Budgeting may sound boring, but you need to work out your costs in advance of creating anything. By understanding exactly how much it will cost to create and how much you need to sell to make it viable, you will be able to make an informed decision on whether to proceed. For example, so many practitioners go full steam ahead to book an event, sell tickets at a discounted rate only to find themselves running the session at a loss. In the excitement, they forgot to allow for the room rent, or the cost of providing refreshments. Costs can easily creep up without you realising, until it is too late.

When working out your prices, make sure you allow for everything that goes into creating your event (or product) and how much it will cost to run it. Once you have this figure, you can work out how much you need to earn just to cover your costs. Do this at the planning stage of your event or product and it will soon show you if there is a problem and you need to rethink what you are doing.

Forecasting

Understanding what you need to sell in each month or quarter will help you understand what you need to do to achieve your annual income goals.

Create a table outlining your different services and products so you have a good understanding of what you need to achieve to earn the income you want. Do this as an overview for the period you are working on. In the example in Table 2, I have based it on one month with 20 client appointments, a taster session, a workshop and a workbook. You will have to pay for your overheads out of the profit so this total will not be your salary.

Table 2: Breakdown of monthly income

Product/service	Price each	Costs each	Number of products/services	Forecast income	Forecast profit
1:1 client appt	£80	£15	16/month	£1280	£1,040
two-hour taster	£25	£75	10 places	£250	£175
two-day workshop	£350	£500	6 places	£2,100	£1,600
Digital workbook	£10	£0	10	£100	£100
Total				**£3,730**	**£2,915**

"You are too expensive!"

Have you experienced that awkward moment when someone you would love to help says "you are too expensive"? They may continue with "the cost is higher than I expected" or "I can get the same cheaper from another practitioner".

Then comes the uncomfortable silence, your heart sinks and you start to question your prices. It is scary and frustrating, but it is something most of us face at some point running our own business. Pricing is such a subjective area, one person's cheap is another person's expensive. One client will put a huge value on your service, whereas another will see it as an extravagance, or think they can get better value elsewhere.

If you try to justify your prices you will find yourself rambling on, getting caught up trying to over-explain your prices. You will find yourself saying how what you do is better and why you charge what you do, and it goes on, and on, and on.

Instead, hold your confidence, agree and wait for their response. If they do not see the value you can always ask why they think you are too expensive. They may have more questions before they make a final decision. They may want your services but do not have the budget right now, so you could offer them other cheaper options.

This is where you can get creative, think about what you can offer people who are not ready to pay for your services and products. Do you have information on your website you can send them links to? Do you give free talks they can attend? Do you have lower-priced workshops or products they can purchase if they are not ready to commit to your premium services?

If you do not have anything suitable you can offer, are there useful videos or resources you can point them towards? Being helpful, even if it is with information from others, will reflect well on you. This person may never work with you but could still be a great ambassador for you.

Should you work for free?

Many practitioners end up giving away far too much for free and can be left feeling drained and undervalued. Whilst you want to help as many people as possible, you will not survive as a business by just doing freebies. Your practice will be a hobby and you will need other income streams to pay your bills.

There are drawbacks to offering freebies and people do not always value them in the same way as they would if they paid for your expertise. Have you done a free talk where only half the people who booked showed up? Have you been asked for advice which was not followed, even when you spent ages helping the person?

Clients are more likely to show up, commit, and take action if they are paying you. Spending time working with people who do not achieve the results will affect your confidence and you need to value your time, if you expect others to.

There are a few situations where it is good to work for free. Whenever you do anything for free in your business it needs to be as a result of a strategic decision. You want to avoid a situation of giving, giving, giving, and hoping something will come back. We look at the strategic ways you can use freebies in your marketing in the next chapter, Marketing basics.

Whenever you offer free work, make sure you have clear boundaries, so everyone involved knows the rules. This will help you avoid doing more and more for free on activities that will not necessarily help you or your business. Limit the amount you give away for free, whether it is a certain number of sessions, 15-minute discovery calls, or a one-hour talk. There is always an opportunity cost to everything you give away for free, every time you say yes to a freebie you are saying no to something else in your business.

EXERCISE: Own your value

You have made a huge investment in time and money to be able to offer the services you do. To help you own your value, work out the cost, and time it has taken you to train and the ongoing costs and requirements of being a practitioner. Write these figures in your notebook as a reminder. This will help you to recognise and reinforce your value to yourself if you feel a little wobbly about your charges.

You have set your prices to match the value you provide to your clients. Keep them written down and displayed somewhere so you can refer to them easily. Having them at hand will make it easier for you to share them as you will just be reading numbers rather than thinking about prices.

TAKEAWAY

Pricing communicates your value as a practitioner and can make or break your business. You need to value your services and charge what you are worth.

CASE STUDY

Name: Vivienne Campbell
Discipline: Medical Herbalist, Forager and Natural Cosmetic Maker
Website: theherbalhub.com

Vivienne qualified as a medical herbalist in 2003 and has made it her full-time career since graduating. She teaches herbal medicine and wild food foraging and is also a professional natural cosmetic-formulator, consultant and teacher. She is an international speaker, presented on television, has been interviewed for documentaries and written articles for journals and specialist publications.

Why did you decide to become a practitioner?

I felt compelled to become a herbalist. I always had an interest in natural medicine because during the Second World War two of my relatives attended a naturopath who helped them both a great deal with very serious medical conditions. I grew up with a respect for natural medicine and eating a whole food diet, so I have always understood the link between food and health.

What is your vision for your business?

I truly believe that it is everyone's birth right to learn how to use some common safe local plants as food and basic medicine. I am passionate about the wonderful therapeutic plants that surround us. I love teaching people, be they professionals or total beginners, how to use herbs simply, effectively and joyfully.

I want to have an ethical and worthwhile business where my life is sustained by my work and my passion. In turn I will be able to teach more people about herbs and do more good in the world, and for the environment. My business needs to be the complete plant, with a root system so that it can sustain itself.

What are the most important things to date that have helped you grow your business?

1. Necessity: my herbal work is my livelihood. I qualified when I was 24 so I didn't have physical or financial resources from a previous career, nor did I have a day job to cover me. I simply had to find a way to make being a herbalist work and cover my living costs. I started by building my clinic and went out giving talks. I worked in a multi-discipline clinic and made friends with the local health food

shop in order to build my connections and establish myself within my local community. I did a lot of clinical work to start with and once I started to get good results for my patients, they sent other people to see me and I got known for my reputation.

2. Adversity forced me to grow and find ways of doing things and adapting in order to survive. I made a commitment to take the work to more people and take the opportunities that came from them. The recession was particularly hard-hitting where I live and largely wiped out my clinical work during that time but this pushed me to find creative new ways to continue to connect people to therapeutic herbs. This changed the focus of my work for the better and in the long-term made it stronger.

3. Passion and integrity. If people are genuine about what they do, have integrity and purpose, then it is highly likely that people will want to work with them, and all sorts of unforeseen and unplanned opportunities will come to them. Be really good at what you do. Working really hard, treating people in my clinic and sharing my passion through workshops and talks led to my biggest marketing opportunities. I was approached to appear on television, be interviewed and asked to speak at events because of my professional and ethical reputation.

   It is important to be able to sustain yourself financially from the good work, so that you do not need to take work from people or companies, or even part-time employment that does not suit your values. I sometimes think the list of people and corporations that I have turned down speaks more about me than the things I actually do.

4. Understanding economic sustainability is as critical to your business as environmental sustainability. Unfortunately, most herbalists are not taught how to work out their costings and prices when they train. They can be resentful of people charging, calling thriving practitioners "business people" in a derogative way and not recognising that there is a huge difference between running a sustainable, ethical business and how large, purely profit-driven corporations operate. The understanding of how money works in business goes through everything from working out how much it costs to set up a dispensary, to having a system to take payments, and charging for anyone who does not show up for an appointment. If practitioners are struggling with this, it is most likely not their fault! It is simply because no-one has

shown them how to do this. Once you can sustain yourself, it gives you options to be charitable and have choices over how you live and work.

With hindsight, is there anything you would have done differently?

I wish I had been taught to charge and run a clinic properly as when I started, I was essentially guessing how much stock cost and how much to charge. I eventually found out from a business coach how to work out my finances to ensure I could build a sustainable business. My clinic would have started very differently if I had known from the beginning.

I wish I had been more open to different opportunities as I only saw the clinic at first, I did not see the potential for other ways to work and how I could really look after myself. It is very hard-going running a full-time medical clinic, you need some lighter work that recharges you e.g. herb walks, product-making etc. If you do not have a team, you need to find a way of balancing the work, so you do not burn out.

What is next for your business?

I have three books to write and I am looking at developing more practitioner training for continual professional development.

CHAPTER TEN

Marketing Basics

M arketing is just telling people what you do and how you can help them. You can have the best service or product in the world but if no-one knows it exists you will not have a business for very long. When it comes down to it marketing is a numbers game, the more people who know about you and your services, the more clients you will attract.

When I studied marketing many moons ago, I learnt people needed to hear about you seven times before they bought from you. Today we are bombarded by marketing from every direction, it is estimated that people may need to hear about you two or three times more than the original seven times! This is where your marketing comes in and helps you build a relationship with your potential clients, so they know you are the right practitioner for them.

Marketing in its simplest terms is sharing your knowledge and offering people the chance to find out more, or to work with you. It does not have to be anything flashy or complicated, you just have to get out there and start sharing.

All the marketing you create should fulfil the following criteria:

- Be helpful to your clients and educate, entertain, or inspire them
- Fit with your brand and the topics you speak about
- Be created for a purpose and has a point to it

Always ask "Why?"

Before you do any marketing activity, always ask yourself why you are doing it. Just because something has become fashionable it does not mean it is the right thing for you. Comparing yourself to others and thinking you should be doing the same can misdirect you, instead you should be focusing on what is right for you.

Recently a practitioner friend decided she wanted a sparkling new website and to start a vlog (video blog). When we talked about why she was doing it, it was because she thought she had to, but she already had a full diary of clients from an established referral system. She is happy with her business as it stands so why did she want an all-singing all-dancing new website? It was because she had seen some lovely websites by new practitioners and had heard you have to make videos. On reflection, they did not add anything to her business other than a lot of work and expense. She had no intention of creating additional income online and was at capacity with her client numbers.

For now, she can be found online through professional directories, on social media, and through her Google My Business page. If, in the future, she changes her mind and wants to do more online, absolutely, she can build an amazing website, but at a time when it will benefit her and her business.

So, before you start the next marketing activity, ask:

- Why am I doing this?
- Does it help me achieve my goals?
- Is this what I really want to spend my time doing?
- Does it make my clients happy?
- Will it attract clients to my practice?

Whilst you should always strive to be visible and market yourself, make sure it is not a knee jerk reaction to something you have seen someone else do. Think about what you want to achieve from the activity and whether it is the best use of your time and resources right now.

Creating your marketing message

Having a clear marketing message makes it easy for people to understand whom you help and how you help them. So often practitioners just describe their discipline, but although you understand what you do, often the person you are speaking to does not. Alternatively, they may have an opinion on what you do which could be totally wrong. Osteopaths are often wrongly thought of as only working with people who have back problems, but this is a tiny proportion of the clients they can help. If people do not understand what you do how will they know you can help them? Why would they pay you?

You need a clear message, one simple enough for a child to understand and repeat. That way, if your offering does not suit someone personally, they will be able to recommend you to a friend in need of your services. Your message is a simple description of what you do, you may have heard it referred to as an "elevator pitch". It is a succinct way to describe what you do and appears consistently throughout your different marketing materials.

The research you did in Chapter 7, Your clients to identify the language they use, how they describe their challenges and the solutions they are looking for will help you craft your message. This research is gold for creating messages that resonate with your favourite clients.

EXERCISE: Your simple marketing message

Craft your message in a similar format to this:

- I help (the people you help) from/with (the problem you solve) to (the results you help them achieve) through/using (your approach)
- Example—I help menopausal women suffering from erratic symptoms to regain their vitality using herbal medicine

The more specific and simple the language you use, the better. Your marketing message is not set in stone, this is your starting point. You will not get it right the first time so be prepared for it to evolve and keep on evolving as you grow.

Deeper messaging

There is another layer to your marketing message which goes deeper. This layer is where you show what makes you different and unique. It is at this level where you really start to attract your favourite clients and repel those who are not a good fit for you.

This area of your messaging weaves throughout everything you do and demonstrates what makes you tick. It shares who you are as a person, what you stand for, and is where you let people into your world to discover the real you. Talk about your values and the things you believe in to attract the right people to your business.

For many practitioners showing this side is scary. You are selling yourself and feel vulnerable, as it feels like you are opening yourself up for criticism. However, this is how you will connect with other like-minded people to build relationships and trust.

For years I fought my inner "Captain Sensible" as I felt it was boring, especially as I worked in marketing. Eventually, experience showed me that this is exactly why clients are attracted to me and it is where my superpowers lie. Absolutely, some people will be put off by it, but they are not the right people for me.

EXERCISE: Crafting your deeper message

Grab your notebook. In Chapter 4 we looked at your "why" and in Chapter 6 we looked at authentic marketing and creating your story. The work you did in both these chapters will come in useful for this exercise.

- What are your core values in life?
- What do you stand for?
- What is your purpose, your cause, your beliefs?
- Why do you do what you do?
- What are the qualities that make you, you?
- Why are people attracted to you? What do they ask you for help with?

Your message is key to your marketing, but it is difficult to refine your message on your own. You can certainly do the groundwork, but you will need to get other opinions to really hone your message. This is an ideal project to work through with a coach or mastermind group.

What you will end up with is extensions to your simple marketing message from earlier in this chapter which you can use for different marketing activities. For example, on your "About you" page on your website, or on a social media profile, you would include deeper messages sharing who you are, what you do, why you do what you do and what you stand for. You will have longer and shorter versions depending on where they are used, but there will be a common theme running throughout.

Case studies and testimonials

People love stories! They are naturally drawn to them and want to know what happens next. Stories are an incredibly powerful way to communicate and illustrate how you help people. A great way to do this in your practice is by using case studies and testimonials.

A case study outlines a client's journey, in order to illustrate their experiences. These can be from an actual client, a hypothetical one, or a hybrid of the two. Testimonials are basically an expression of thanks or a statement of recommendation.

Your clients' success stories are a huge asset to your business. They provide potential clients with powerful marketing messages and assist them in deciding whether to work with you or not.

People like to know exactly how you can help them. Understanding how you helped others is a brilliant way to demonstrate this. This will help to alleviate any fears potential clients have around taking the next step with you and provide you with credibility.

They can be used in any of your marketing activities, to reinforce messages and points you make. They are especially important on your website where they provide proof of your effectiveness to the visitor.

What to include

The ideal testimonial or case study needs to demonstrate three main things:

- Why your client wanted to work with you
- What issue(s) you helped them with and how you did this
- What difference working with you made to them and the results they achieved

Avoid using the testimonials that are just complimenting you on how amazing you are. Of course I love to hear: "Helen was fabulous!", but that says absolutely nothing about how I actually helped my client and will not do anything to support my business.

Collecting case studies and testimonials

Start by identifying clients who you have a great relationship with and you think will be happy to share their story. If a client drops you an email to thank you and let you know how they are doing ask permission to use it for your marketing. A story written in your client's own words may not be a literary masterpiece, but their choice of language will resonate with other potential clients. If they have included something that does not fit with your ethical guidelines or code of conduct, suggest changes and send it back to your client for approval, prior to publishing. If someone provides a written testimonial, ask if they are happy to include a photo as this provides another layer of credibility.

You can protect your client's identity by using only their first name, using their initials, or giving them a different name (although for transparency, mention this). This is particularly important if the work you do is of a sensitive nature, as your client will want to feel safe sharing any story.

Ensure your clients do not feel pressured or obligated to provide a testimonial for you. In my experience, satisfied clients are more than happy to share their experience, but it has to be their choice.

Traditionally, many testimonials and case studies were written. With the ownership of smartphones and other accessible technologies, clients may find it easier to produce video or audio testimonials. These hold incredible power as they provide a real person for potential clients to relate to.

Another option is to interview a client once they have finished working with you. This can be in person, remotely, on video, audio recording, or taking notes. By taking on the creation of the case study or testimonial yourself, you are increasing the chance of client participation. All you are asking your client for is a little bit of their time. If you do this, always show the finished piece to your client and get their written agreement that they are happy for it to be shared.

Be careful about what you publish. Make sure it fits with the guidelines of your professional body as many have very strict rules on the use of case studies and testimonials. Be reasonable about what you include and ensure you (or your client) are not making any claims that cannot be substantiated if challenged. In the UK, we have to abide by the Advertising Standards Authority (ASA) who are an independent regulator and set the rules for advertising. The Committee of Advertising Practice (CAP) is responsible for writing the advertising codes outlining what you can and cannot claim in your marketing.

For every client story you have, keep a note of their contact details and their written permission for using it. GDPR requires you to have permission for exactly how, when, and for how long any data is kept which includes testimonials.

Have a process

Create the habit of requesting testimonials once a client has finished working with you. The best time to ask is when they still feel motivated by the results they got and fully remember the experience of working with you. If you leave it too long, they will get busy with life and you may miss the opportunity.

What if I do not have testimonials?

You may just be starting out as a new practitioner or limited on what you can publish due to your professional governing body. In either situation, consider doing a hypothetical case study (professional body permitting) to demonstrate the journey of a client working with you. Ask people you practised on as a student (outside of your training establishment) if they are willing to give you a testimonial for the work you did with them. You could also request endorsements from your colleagues or employers to provide evidence of your capabilities and credibility.

Offering freebies

Whilst you should value your time and be paid for your work, there are certain situations where you will benefit from working for free, but this should always be done strategically and for limited periods of time. Here are some of the strategic reasons for offering freebies:

Starting your business. Offering free sessions can be a great way to get your business moving if you are just starting out. Giving away a limited number of appointments in exchange for testimonials will help you build your confidence and provide you with client stories to use in your marketing.

Launching new projects. If you are in the process of launching a new project or service, free samples, taster sessions, or beta testing are all good options. They will allow you to develop your skills, give you experience of delivering your service, provide feedback to help you iron out any issues, and you can collect testimonials for your website. If you decide to do this, make sure you set it for a limited time period, or number. Use it as a learning strategy to grow from and offer full-priced services following on from it.

Authors often offer their new book for free as an eBook for a limited amount of time. This way they kickstart the number of downloads online and receive reviews to help raise their profile which may result in more sales.

Charitable work. If you have a charity or cause which is special to you it is great to support them. You need to decide in advance how you will do this and clearly communicate it to those involved. Ideas include offering a specific number of free appointments, making a regular donation, fundraising, or mentoring new practitioners. This may not bring you clients directly but will help you raise your profile, build strong relationships, and fulfil your personal goals.

Small events. Hosting small events such as workshops, talks, and taster sessions are a great way to build relationships with potential clients. It gives people the opportunity to meet you in person, experience how you work, and find out how you can potentially help them.

Get creative with these events. There are lots of different opportunities to get seen and share your knowledge in your local area. To help build my business as a practitioner I held stands at local fairs, ran talks, spoke at events, and participated in clinic open evenings.

Swapping services. If you need help with a problem and you have someone who has those skills and needs your help, there is no reason why you should not help each other out. Make sure it is a fair swap with similar value services or products. The last thing you want is for one side to feel that they got a bad deal.

Swapping services with another practitioner it is a good way for you to understand each other's discipline. This will give both of you the confidence to refer clients to each other in the future.

Good PR opportunity. If you are going to do free work look for opportunities to help build your business and attract new clients to your door. It must be worth your time, do not provide freebies just for the sake of it.

As a practitioner, I have worked with journalists who then wrote about their experience with me and as a result of the articles I gained several new clients. The free sessions were more than paid for by the exposure my clinic received and the new clients who booked to work with me.

Handling requests for free work

Setting good boundaries is key to protecting your time and resources. Decide ahead of time what you are willing to give away and make sure you write it down in your notebook, so you have it to refer to. Make sure everyone else in the relationship is aware of the boundaries too so you are all clear about exactly what you are providing in order to avoid any difficult conversations later.

If you regularly receive questions by email asking for free advice, construct a way of handling it that does not take too much time. If it is something that is frequently asked, write a blog to address it and send a link, or create an email template you can copy and paste. Writing an individual in-depth response by email can take you 30 minutes. Instead, you could offer a free 15-minute discovery call and a link to your diary. You will be surprised how many people do not bother booking a call as it is too much trouble. They would, however, be happy with you emailing them a lengthy response.

Helping people for free without draining yourself

You will always get people who ask for your advice and never expect to pay. For these people, think about practical ways you can share information without taking up your time or energy.

As a practitioner, I created a series of 50 podcasts with a colleague which provided great value and can be downloaded free of charge. I also wrote hundreds of articles which people are welcome to help themselves to. It feels good to be able to provide a service to those who want my help but are not ready to commit to, or pay for, working with me directly.

Other ideas could be videos, online courses, templates, or eBooks, basically anything that can be provided with minimal effort once created but provides a quick and easy way to respond to initial enquiries or requests for information. Being generous is a great quality but when it comes to your time and energy it needs to be done strategically.

Building a business with conversation

Have you noticed websites often have chat boxes that pop up asking if they can help you? This is called conversational marketing and it is all about building relationships with customers. Whilst technology is behind this idea, the simplicity of building your business through the power of conversations is very effective.

When marketing is too structured and scheduled it can appear cold and impersonal, and will not attract clients. Whilst you absolutely need to be visible and make offers, it is easier to do it one conversation at a time. Building your business this way allows you to really get to know your clients. It also allows them to understand how you can help them and to build a solid, trusting relationship.

This one-to-one approach will help you learn about your clients and build a better experience for them in the long term.

Be human. As humans, we have a basic desire to connect with each other. We are strong when we have a community where we feel supported and heard. Using conversations as a way of marketing yourself will allow people to experience the real you and be attracted (or not, but that is okay) to the natural, authentic you. It is such a simple but powerful strategy and just requires you to be you!

Be helpful. As a practitioner, you want to help people, it is what you do! Allowing yourself to have useful conversations, sharing how you help your clients is gold for your business. Do not go into every conversation looking for clients although you need to make sure you can articulate simply what you do and whom you help using your marketing message.

Get chatting. Take time to talk to people whether it is chatting to a shop assistant or to someone at a conference. Be interested in what they say rather than trying to make yourself interesting. Your opportunity to share what you do will come and you will learn loads by just listening.

Respond to comments. Conversations can happen in many different formats, from online or over the phone to in person. Make sure if you are posting anything online, you respond to comments, just as you would in person. This will not only help your profile, but it will also assist in building relationships. Time is of the essence and people expect to get their questions answered quickly. Speedy replies to emails and other communications will work in your favour. If you are not available to reply let people know when to expect a response, to avoid disappointment.

Many big companies are adopting conversational marketing as they realise connection is a really great way to improve their sales. Answering questions, listening to feedback, and finding new ways to solve problems comes from having real conversations.

How much marketing should you do?

Practitioners often worry they can do too much marketing and will come across as too pushy. You only notice everything you do because you are creating it and you are living and breathing it. Your audience on the other hand, will only see a fraction of your efforts. If you feel completely comfortable about the amount of marketing you are doing, then you are not doing enough to get the results you want.

Ultimately there is no right or wrong answer, but the more time you commit to marketing your practice (assuming you are working on the right things) the quicker your business will grow.

While you are waiting to fill your diary with appointments use un-booked time slots to concentrate on your marketing activities. For example, if you want to see ten clients a week for an hour each and you only have three booked in, invest the other seven hours in working on your marketing, in addition to your scheduled time.

SABOTEUR ALERT: Resistance to marketing

You know how it feels, you do some marketing for your practice and start to progress, and then comes the resistance and you get side-tracked. You know logically you have to keep marketing yourself to build a thriving practice, but it feels like an uphill battle at times.

Resistance is just your subconscious way of trying to keep you safe and protected. Our brains are wired to anticipate anything that may be uncomfortable and move us away from it. Anything that pushes you outside of your comfort zone will trigger fear.

Fear of the unknown, fear of failure, fear of success, fear of being visible, fear of any kind will make the journey more challenging and cause resistance.

By accepting the situation that your brain is just trying to keep you comfortable and safe, you can address the resistance that is occurring. Write down any fears that come up as this will help to stop them from whirling around in your head. Seeing them written down in black and white can be freeing, especially when you realise exactly what is keeping you stuck. It is a great way to gain perspective. Use your support network and preferred personal development methods to help you work through this.

TAKEAWAY

Always ask yourself why you are doing marketing activities and make sure they are for the right reasons. Have a clear marketing message so you know how to communicate what you do easily and succinctly in a way people will understand.

CHAPTER ELEVEN

Making Marketing Fun

Fun reduces stress and increases your creativity. If you enjoy something you are much more likely to do it! Fun is good for you, so how can you make your marketing more of a fun activity?

Many practitioners think of marketing as some sort of dark art. It has a reputation for being sleazy or pushy. The get rich quick strategies or one-size-fits-all blueprints are not right for most small businesses, let alone practitioners. Many of these formulas will not sit well with your values and certainly will not be your idea of fun.

Instead focus your marketing around sharing, being helpful, and playing to your strengths. Modern marketing is about connecting with people, empathy, and building relationships. The best marketing will connect you with your favourite clients in a way you both enjoy and it will not feel like marketing to either of you.

Think of all the different types of marketing you experience in your day. Which campaigns make you stop and think? How do you like to consume information from your favourite brands?

I love podcasts and listen to them when I am driving. You may prefer reading, watching videos, or infographics, there are many different options and many will not feel like marketing because you are being entertained, educated, or inspired. How you like to consume marketing content will give you ideas for what you could create for your prospective clients.

Having fun should not be the opposite of marketing, it should be part of it! You are far more likely to keep something up when you are enjoying it. You will get better results and connect with people when you allow your personality to shine through.

A practitioner friend of mine is also an amazing calligrapher. She produces the most beautiful quotes for her social media accounts. It is her hobby and something she finds fun and easy to do. It provides her potential clients with inspirational works of art as well as a little window into her world.

EXERCISE: What is fun for you?

This exercise builds on your personal mind map from Chapter 3 Reality check, grab your notebook and write down all the things you love doing, using these questions as prompts:

- What are your hobbies outside of work?
- Are you a social animal or do you love spending time alone?
- What lights you up and puts a big smile on your face?

Marketing to your strengths

There is often a struggle when it comes to knowing where to start with marketing your practice and which strategies to choose. We are bombarded with all the different things we think we should be doing and can find ourselves easily side-tracked and jumping around from one thing to another. If you are currently struggling to get momentum with marketing your practice, it is time to review what you are doing and work out whether it is a good fit for you.

The simplicity of marketing to your strengths will allow you to start understanding what is working, rather than trying 15 different things with little or no results. Focusing on your marketing strengths will help you find your marketing flow and make life (and marketing) much easier.

EXERCISE: Your communication strengths

What form of communication do you find easiest and works best with your personality? How do you best communicate with people? Are you a talker, a writer, do you love performing, or expressing yourself through art and design?

Write in your notebook your communication strengths, considering what you are best at and what you find easiest to do. Now compare this to the things you find fun and identify any marketing activities you could do which would combine them.

Activities based on strengths

As you recognise the most effective way you communicate you can consider your options for creating your marketing. Whatever your communication strengths, there will be a number of options available to you. You do not have to do everything; you need to pick the activity that works best for you and start communicating with your clients. Here are a few examples of the different options to get you thinking:

- **Writing:** blogging, books, guides, workbooks, newsletters, email marketing, magazine articles, magazine columns, social media posts, or submit guest posts for other websites
- **Talking:** podcasting, networking, talks, speaking engagements, radio, or podcast interviews and webinars
- **Video:** vlogging, video series, TV interviews, webinars, video interviews, video courses and live video
- **Images:** social media images, infographics, photographs, cartoons, illustrations, and animated video

Communicating with your ideal clients

Now consider where your clients hang out and the type of marketing that would appeal to them. The crossover between what you like doing and what you are good at, and where your clients are and how they like to consume information is the ideal place to focus your marketing efforts. By identifying marketing opportunities that combine these elements, you will make your marketing fun and you are more likely to be consistent with it.

For example, if you work with small business owners on managing stress, and you are a social animal who likes talking, you could go networking. If you work with new mums wanting to use natural baby products, and are a home bird who likes video and editing films, you could create a vlog.

Keep it simple

Do not get carried away with all the things you think you should be doing. This will keep you jumping around from one thing to another and not achieving anything.

Focus on two or three main activities that will help you grow your business. If you are just getting started, you need to make sure you have the foundations in place, so it may be activities like creating your brand, building a website, and reaching out to your personal network. If you are more established, it may mean recording a podcast, attending local networking events, or running free talks. The choice is yours!

It is better to do a few activities well and consistently than adopt a scattergun approach, trying lots of different things but not giving anything a chance to work. Once you get into the habit of creating consistent marketing with a couple of elements, you can add to them. See your marketing as planting seeds, you must nurture them to help them grow. Most marketing activities are long-term strategies and will help you create a thriving sustainable practice for the future.

TAKEAWAY

Having fun should not be the opposite of marketing, it should part of it.

CASE STUDY

Name: Geoff Nicholson
Discipline: Performance and Mindset Specialist
Website: geoffnicholson.uk

Geoff is a coach and mentor helping entrepreneurs and holisticpreneurs across the world to build a business that brings them joy and success. He is an international speaker and hosts a podcast "Success IQ" where he invites other thought and business leaders from around the world to share their journey and challenges in becoming successful and living a fulfilled life.

Why did you decide to become a practitioner?

Having fully recovered from my own version of hell with debilitating mental and physical conditions, I wanted to help people be the best versions of themselves. People have way more potential than they think and I help them to smash through the brick wall of desperation and take them on the journey to inspiration.

What is your vision for your business?

My family laugh about "Geoff's Empire". I want to inspire and assist two million people by providing them with simple and effective strategies to create great businesses, great lives and have fun both online and offline.

What are the most important things to date that have helped you grow your business?

1. Having the courage to be vulnerable about my own challenges and to be prepared to be wrong and look the idiot. The willingness to go "I don't know" and ask questions. People relate to and warm to it and it allows for an extra level of authenticity.
2. My willingness to have fun and learn. Being dyslexic and feeling nervous about putting words on paper, being labelled by teachers as not being good, being ill; I learnt getting better was all about fun. Clients teach me something new each day and I always come from a place of wanting to know more, having fun and learning more. Being able to laugh at stuff is critical.
3. Build the best badass support structure around me that I could. Having family and friends who will support what I do even if they do not totally get it. Having a great coach on my back and being part of a mastermind group who support and challenge me and do not allow me to get away with any nonsense. Having them brings me back on course when I need it.

With hindsight, is there anything you would have done differently?

Yes, I would do half the things I am doing now, earlier! I was never going to achieve perfection, but I would try and wait until everything was perfect. My podcast would have been started two years earlier, my speaking gigs would have started earlier too. My inner critic gets very loud around this stuff and launching things, which has stopped things happening.

What is next for your business?

1. Community—I want to build a strong community around a Facebook group with a membership site to take "Geoff the coach" and make it digital to help more people.
2. Book—I will finish writing my book and publish it, it is the best business card you can have to open doors for you.

CHAPTER TWELVE

Selling from the Heart

Selling is not something that comes naturally to most practitioners. They often feel it is manipulative and requires a brash and bullish approach in order to make a sale. True, there are some people out there whose style is to shout about their offerings, pushing them onto you without even knowing whether you are interested. Unfortunately, this is how most practitioners view selling, but it does not have to be like this.

Selling does not have to be pushy, but you do have to make sales to survive. It is necessary if you want to earn enough money to pay your bills by working as a practitioner. If not, your business will not be viable, and you will be forced to find another source of income to subsidise yourself or cease practising altogether.

Ultimately, selling is just about helping people solve problems by making them offers. It does not have to be more complicated than that. You make offers to people based on how you can help them. By making offers, you will start to train your clients to understand the value of your services and products.

Fortunately, there are ways of selling which are filled with integrity. There are different ways of making offers based on mutual respect for your clients and for your products and services, you just need to find the right style for you.

Helpful marketing

The need for selling is reduced if you create helpful marketing. This is a perfect strategy for practitioners as it fits brilliantly with the ethos of wanting to help people. It will also limit the need to adopt a hard sale approach as people will be prompted to approach you instead. Helpful marketing is about creating lots of value and building relationships and connections with your clients and prospective clients.

Helpful marketing will help you build sustainability for your business by helping people first, once they are ready to work with someone, you are first in line. By building these relationships, your potential clients will already have a connection with you and trust that when you do make them an offer it is based on what is best for them.

Making offers

Whilst consistently helping people with free sessions, producing lots of helpful articles, or answering endless email enquiries is honourable, you still have to make offers. You have to tell people that you have a solution to their problem. If not, you will build a community of clients around you who are consuming all your free information without even realising you have a solution for sale. Making offers is the missing piece in the puzzle to build a thriving practice for most practitioners, and it is a critical one.

There will be times where you make offers and people will say "no" and that is okay. It may not be the right time for them, or you may not have the solution they are looking for. These are the times you need to put down to experience, brush yourself down and move on. With every no, you are one step closer to a yes. The more you practice making offers, the easier it will be and the more success you will achieve.

Keep it simple, you are not pushing yourself on people, you are simply saying, if you want to resolve your issue, I have this solution available.

Follow-up

How many prospective clients are missing out on working with you, just because you have not kept yourself on their radar?

Most practitioners focus their marketing efforts on attracting new clients to their door. They forget about the potential clients who have already enquired and expressed an interest in their services or products.

Marketing's focus is to fill your practice with amazing clients. If you are getting interest but it is not converting into paying clients, your problem is not your marketing. Spending more time and money on marketing to fill your practice will not work if you are not following up on the interest you have generated and making offers to these people.

You need to create a follow-up system that works for you and fits with your style of communication. Having a checklist as a reminder of each step will help you to implement it with every enquiry you receive.

An example checklist for a website enquiry is:

- Receive an enquiry about your services through your website.
- Answer the enquiry and offer them a phone call to discuss their requirements and tell them about your solution.
- Make a note in your diary to follow them up in a week if you have not heard back from them.
- Send a helpful email asking if they have any questions about your services? Is there any more information they need? Send them a link to your free guide and make them an offer to join your email list.
- Keep in touch with them through your regular emails or newsletter (if they signed up for them) making relevant offers.
- If they have not signed up for your email list, make a note in your diary to follow them up in two weeks with links to useful information relevant to their enquiry and where they can sign-up to your email list. Offer them another opportunity for a phone call.

Your checklist will vary depending on where the enquiry came from, for example connecting with someone you met networking as opposed to someone who contacted you through your website will elicit a different follow-up response. Adding a follow-up system to your marketing efforts which is tailored to how the initial enquiry was generated will help you to connect with potential clients in a more personalised way and will help build relationships faster. Follow-up of some sort, regardless of how simple it is, is better than waiting for clients to remember to call you!

Tell clients the next step

Make sure clients understand the process of how to work with you and the steps they need to take. The clearer you can make the system, and the easier it is for them to navigate, the more clients you will get. For example, having an online diary they can book through. Get a friend to review the journey of working with you to ensure it makes sense and it is as simple as possible.

Understanding your client journey

There are ways of assisting the sales process by guiding clients through the steps they need to take in order to achieve the results they are looking for. Your client journey is simply the route they take from discovering you, to working with you.

Once you start seeing clients, they already follow a path whether you realise it or not. Having clarity over this will help you focus your marketing efforts in the right places and make offers at the right time.

Attract attention. How do people discover you in the first place? What marketing are you doing to reach the people who do not know you exist? This marketing is about building awareness of who you are and how you help people. Start asking new clients how they heard about you as this will give you a good indication of what marketing is working.

Engage. At this stage, you are turning strangers you have attracted into potential clients who want to work with you. This is where you start making offers of how you can help them.

Delight. Clients who have amazing experiences from working with you will become your best marketers. They will tell people about you which will attract more clients to your practice for you to engage with. They are also the most likely people to want to work with you again, so you need to maintain this relationship and continue to make them offers.

An example of a client journey is:

- Attract attention through social media posts
- Interact with comments and offer them your free guide and to join your email list
- Email marketing to build a relationship and provide helpful information
- Offer free discovery call for your coaching services
- Book call to understand client needs and offer your solution
- Book appropriate package for client
- Continue to email and interact on social media

EXERCISE: Map out your client journey

Plot out your client journey and note down all the points where someone interacts with you. If you are yet to start working with clients, imagine what this journey will be. Start at the beginning when someone first discovers you and review all the different touch points as you go. List the marketing you do in each of these areas and note where you make offers of any kind.

SABOTEUR ALERT: Fear of rejection

Let us face it, there will be times when someone says no to your offer. You reject offers all the time so what makes this different? It is because it is personal to you, it makes it feel so much worse. Marketing is a numbers game and there will be many more people who say no to your offers than say yes. Not everyone is a good fit for you or ready to work with you, and that is okay. If you are scared to make an offer because someone may say no, you will not get to help the people who are waiting and ready for you. Every no will move you a step closer to a yes.

- Build confidence in your abilities and review your answers from the exercise confidence boost in Chapter 2.
- Keep a list of your offerings, including your prices, so you can read them confidently when asked.

TAKEAWAY

You must be selling to have a viable business. Keep it simple and make people offers of services and products that will genuinely help them.

CHAPTER THIRTEEN

Marketing Recipe

Imagine you are throwing a dinner party; your guests are your focus when it comes to picking a menu. Your menu will comprise a few different dishes and you want your guests to leave the party feeling satisfied and happy. Whilst you are looking to please your guests with your food, the recipes you cook will be based on your skills in the kitchen, your tastes, and the availability of ingredients.

Having a menu and following a recipe helps you to keep on track when you are creating your feast and ensures you have the right ingredients available and take the right steps in the right order. Once you start cooking you get creative and tweak the recipes as you go to make them just right. You may even swap one ingredient for another when you realise it does not quite work, this is just part of the process.

You follow the same process when you create your marketing plans, only without the food! To start with, we will create a simple overview plan for your year ahead outlining what you need to do to achieve your goals. This is your menu and includes the products and services you offer your clients. We will then select the marketing strategies (recipes) to suit you and your resources (ingredients) and formulate it in a way you can follow (steps) and replicate as required. Over time you will adjust and change recipes and ingredients to suit you, but you will have a plan and know what you are aiming to achieve and the steps to take.

The simple plan

A common misconception about business and marketing plans is they are long and complicated documents, but it does not have to be like this. There is certainly a time and a place for long detailed plans, for example if you are looking for funding to set up a practice. However, as a practitioner you should aim to keep things simple. A plan is your menu and its recipes, and the focus it gives you will keep you moving forward. Having one is certainly better than not having one and it will give you a far better chance of succeeding. Without one, there are too many ways to get side-tracked and end up aimlessly drifting along, finding yourself in the same place a year from now, wishing things were different.

In its simplest terms a plan, whether a business or marketing plan, is just a cycle and considers the following:

Where am I now? You have already covered this in Chapter 3, Reality check. You need to understand your current situation even if you do not want to admit to yourself how bad things are, burying your head in the sand will not improve matters. If you have not done it yet, take some time to understand where your business is right now, including the scary finances. This will help you decide what activities you need to do first and whether you have the budget to invest in extra help, or technology.

Where do I want to be? You set out your vision in Chapter 4, Creating your dream practice, which will provide you with direction for your business and life. This will help you to identify the long-term goals you want to achieve to realise your vision. It also helps you work out whom you want to work with, how you want to help them, and the rewards you want to receive. You then create smaller, individual goals to help you achieve the larger ones and ultimately live the life you are dreaming about.

How am I going to get there? Taking each of the goals, work out your plan for what you need to do in order to achieve them. You will then create individual recipes which outline the ingredients you need, and the steps to follow which you can then replicate as required. It will help you keep focused and organised, and create the marketing you need to achieve your goals.

How will I know when I have arrived? Marketing is an ongoing process that requires monitoring and adjusting depending on the results achieved just like tasting and tweaking a recipe. You will understand if people are responding to your marketing by their engagement with you: booking appointments, making purchases, or whichever outcome goal you set out to achieve.

Yearly overview

You know what you want to achieve in your business in the long term after setting out your vision in Chapter 4, Creating your dream practice. Use your vision as a compass for where you want to get to and decide what you need to achieve during the next year in order to accomplish it. These will become your yearly goals which will be too big and scary to tackle in one go, so break them down further into smaller achievable goals, creating quarterly goals and monthly goals. These will include the dishes on your menu such as the number of one-to-one clients, workshops, retreats for example as well as any plans you have for launching a video series or writing a book.

Then plot your goals over the next year so you have an overview of what you need to achieve and when. Also include in your overview other information that will affect your business such as:

- Events you are attending
- Relevant key dates
- Annual holidays and celebrations
- Personal holidays, you will need to accommodate these in your plans, especially if you work alone

Having an overview of your year will help you maximise any opportunities to build your business and make sure you are organised for them. You then set your marketing recipes to help you achieve them. See Table 3 for an example of a yearly overview.

Table 3: Yearly overview

QUARTER 1	QUARTER 2
January (New Year) *20 client appointments*	**April (Easter)** *One-week holiday* *20 client appointments* *Workshop: beta test to 8 clients*
February *20 client appointments* *Workshop: start promoting*	**May** *24 client appointments* *Workshop: update following beta test* *Podcast: start promoting*
March (Spring Equinox) *20 client appointments* *Workshop: promote*	**June (Summer Solstice)** *24 client appointments* *Podcast: start weekly show*

QUARTER 3	QUARTER 4
July *Two-weeks holiday* *12 client appointments* *Workshop: start promoting*	**October** *28 client appointments* *Christmas gifts: promote* *Speaking at conference*
August *24 client appointments* *Workshop: promote*	**November** *28 client appointments* *Christmas gifts: Promote* *Attend conference*
September (Autumnal Equinox) *24 client appointments* *Workshop: run for 20 clients* *Christmas gifts: start promoting*	**December (Winter Solstice)** *one-week holiday* *18 client appointments* *Christmas gifts: sale*

EXERCISE: Your yearly overview plan

Using the example in Table 3, work out an overview for the year ahead for your business. You do not have to start in January, just work out what you want to do and when for the next 12 months. Plans are fluid documents and will change over time but having one will help you to keep moving forward in your business. You can download a template for your yearly overview plan at helenharding.co.uk/bonus.

Follow these steps to work out the next 12 months in your business:

1. Vision for your business—where you want to be in five or ten years from now from Chapter 4, Creating your dream practice.
2. What do you need to achieve in the next year in order to realise your vision?
3. Break the year goals down into smaller achievable quarterly goals, and then monthly goals.
4. Set an overview of the year for yourself so you can see what is happening and when. This will help you to get organised, work out if you are being realistic with your goals, and help you to stay on track for the year.

Creating your recipe

Whenever you create any marketing you do it with your favourite client in mind. As we have already established, marketing to your favourite client does not stop you from working with others, but it will ensure your messages speak directly to them. In Chapter 7, Your clients, you identified those you are going to be focusing on and marketing to. Having clarity over whom you are targeting and what action you want them to take from your marketing activities is a starting point.

Even though you know who your favourite clients are, they will be at different stages of being ready to work with you. You need to bear this in mind when you decide on the recipes you are creating for them and the marketing you will be producing.

Practitioners who need to find clients quickly will often focus their marketing efforts in the wrong place, for example on strategies that build awareness such as social media. Most marketing strategies take time to mature and deliver results, which will not help if you need to fill your diary now. These long-term strategies are like planting seeds, you must nurture and tend to them so they grow and blossom into something worthwhile. If you throw a few seeds in the ground you may get lucky and they germinate, but you are not going to get the abundant harvest you want. Whilst you need to be creating awareness to help your business become sustainable and thrive in the long term, it will not find you clients quickly. You need a different marketing approach.

Do you remember playing the children's game "hot and cold"? Someone hides an item and then you look for it with guidance on how close you are to finding it by being told how "hot" or "cold" you are. Hear "cold" and you know you are nowhere near, "hot" on the other hand meant you are on the verge of finding it. This is the same with clients and their readiness for working with you. Not everyone is ready to work with you at this moment in time. They are at different stages and your marketing needs to reflect this and will be different depending on whom you are trying to communicate with.

Hot leads

These are the people most likely to work with you now. They are the people you already have a relationship with and who already know, like, and trust you. This group includes clients you have already worked with and their network. Past and present clients are more likely to work with you now and are far easier to reach than trying to find new ones. It is important you continue to nurture your relationship with this group as they will support your business growth and are more likely to provide you with referrals.

This group also includes people who have recently enquired about your services. They already know who you are, what you do, and are showing an interest in working with you.

If you need clients now, personal connection is by far the quickest way to get clients but, unfortunately, it is also the strategy most resisted by practitioners. Whilst this is the most labour-intensive strategy, it is incredibly powerful and is done in person with a phone call, email, or direct messaging. It does not have to be pushy, just making contact for an update is a great way to remind people you are there to help them. Personal outreach will simply remind someone who is busy to book an appointment with you.

You can also ask current clients for referrals if you have finished working with them and want to find other clients just like them. Most people who are satisfied with the service they have received will be happy to refer you to a friend.

If you are just starting out, reach out to your personal network, explaining whom you help, what you can help them with, and ask them to refer you to anyone they know. These people already know, like, and trust you, even if they have not experienced working directly with you. They will be happy to refer you based on their knowledge of you as a person.

The sort of marketing activities for hot leads includes personal emails, phone calls, meeting up in person, direct messages, handwritten cards and letters.

Warm leads

These are the people who already know you and engage with you at some level. They may open your emails, or comment on your social media posts, but are yet to work with you. You are building a relationship with them and getting to know if you are a good fit for each other. They are likely to move towards working with you at some point in the future, but not quite yet.

With this group, you are using your marketing to reinforce your value and explain how you can help them. Continue to build a connection with this group through your marketing with videos, podcasts, open days, emails, social media, speaking, or networking. You are reinforcing what you do and being helpful until they are ready to work with you.

Cold leads

These people do not know you exist yet or are only just discovering you. At this point, they are not aware of how you can help them, and as you can imagine these are the people least likely to work with you right now. At this stage, your marketing is about building awareness and being helpful. You are introducing people to your world, but they have to get to know you, so they are very early in their journey to work with you.

Imagine your favourite restaurant. Their hot leads are the loyal customers who love their food, return regularly and tell their friends about it. Their warm leads are the people passing by and who read the menu in the window but are yet to book a table. The cold leads are the people who have either walked straight past without noticing it, or if they did see it they have not looked in yet.

With cold leads, you are helping them to find out about you and understand your area of expertise. The types of marketing which build awareness are social media posts, advertising, published work, content marketing, speaking, guest blogging, being interviewed, or having stands at shows or fairs. You are letting people know of your existence and how helpful you are.

There are many crossovers in the activities you do when marketing to hot, warm or cold leads. By having clients who are ready to work with you now and people who are warming up in the background to work with you in the future, you will build a flow of clients and create a sustainable business.

EXERCISE: Hot, warm, and cold leads

Grab your notebook and make three lists: your hot, warm, and cold leads. Include everyone you can think of such as clients you have worked with (or practised with if you are new), enquiries you have received, different groups you are a member of, or groups you can join where your favourite clients hang out, your email subscribers, social media connections, and anyone else you can think of. Work out where you think each person or group is in terms of the stage of readiness to work with you and put them on the relevant list.

Your recipes

You want to create marketing that satisfies your existing clients but which also encourages potential clients to take the next step towards working with you. Your chosen marketing strategies will be different depending on how quickly you need to attract clients to your business and where they are in terms of their readiness to work with you. There is no point doing lots of different marketing activities that do not complement each other or interest your clients. Blindly following other practitioner's marketing activities can lead to this. By choosing marketing recipes to delight your clients whilst working to your strengths, you can keep your marketing simple and cut out a lot of unnecessary work.

Your recipes will combine the ingredients and steps to create your marketing activities to build awareness and relationships, and ultimately sell your products and services. They will constantly evolve and will be chosen based on you, your taste, your skills and what you have available to you. Always start where you are and work out what you can do with what you already have. You may find some recipes need tweaking because you do not have the full list of ingredients available. You can decide if it is a good use of your resources to buy what is missing or whether to swap them for something else.

This is where you can get creative with your marketing just as you would in your cooking. You will start to see what works for you and what is missing, where you need help and what you need to change.

Keep everything as simple as possible as there are so many different marketing strategies to choose from it is easy to get overwhelmed. You have one expert telling you to get on social media, the next telling you to use this software, agencies offering you the promise of great things, it is no wonder you often do not know where to start. Before you know it you are on a shopping spree, trying out freebies and buying the promise of a new and shiny approach, most of which will not even get used. Then they sit there, clogging up your inbox and brain until you have forgotten about them, or they expire.

Therefore, before you go shopping it is important that you have a recipe with a list of the ingredients you need, and you stick to it. There will always be other options you can use and you can try them out when you are ready, but many will have no place in the recipe you are creating now. Once you have your recipe stick to it and only change it or the ingredients when you know they are not working, or you need to bring another flavour to the dish to make it work.

Testing

As you would with a cooking recipe, you need to test your marketing as you go to make sure it is working. Some things will work first time, others will not but the more you understand what works and where your clients come from the more you can focus your efforts on the right marketing activities. You will get a sense of whether things are working if people are engaging with your marketing and you are starting to build relationships with people. A growing email list, more visitors to your website or more sales of your products and services are all good signs of a successful marketing campaign.

For example asking new clients how they heard of you, will help you to identify what is working in your marketing so you can focus on these activities and phase out the activities that do not seem to yield any results.

Most marketing strategies focus on the long term and you may not see results straight away; it takes time to build momentum. Just doing something once or twice is not enough to know if it works, you need to give it a chance. Once you have been marketing yourself consistently for at least three months reflect on what is working by looking at your numbers, if you are not seeing any growth it is time for a rethink. Even if you spent a long time setting something up it is not worth the effort of continuing with it if it does not work.

Example of a recipe with ingredients and steps

Keep your recipe really simple and restrict yourself to one page:

What is my goal?
• To increase the number of one-hour clinical appointments by five a week to ten, doubling my income to £800 per week by the end of June.

Who is my ideal client?
• Stressed-out professionals who struggle to sleep and do not want to become reliant on pills but instead find a natural way to achieve restful and restorative sleep.

What am I offering them?
• One-to-one herbal medicine appointments.

What are my recipes?

1. Personal email (hot leads)
   • List of hot leads
   • Create email templates
      ◦ Using my list of hot leads, write personalised emails to three people every day
      ◦ Track responses and email a follow-up to those who have not replied after a week
2. Networking (warm and cold leads)
   • Identify local networking groups
   • Create a useful leaflet on sleep to give away including contact details
   • Create a follow-up process
   • Create a talk
      ◦ Contact organisers and offer to give talks
      ◦ Attend two meetings a month
      ◦ Follow-up all contacts made with an email and connect with them on social media

3. Social media (hot, warm and cold leads)
   - Focus on LinkedIn
   - Write articles on sleep
   - Identify relevant groups to network in
     - Create useful posts with tips and questions on sleep, and share three times a week
     - Respond to comments every day
     - Share and comment on other people's posts every day

Is it working or do i need to change something? Your numbers will help you to determine whether your recipe is working and if you are making progress towards achieving your goal. Track them each month and you will soon see if you need to make any changes to your recipe.

EXERCISE: Your marketing recipe

Use the following format and create a recipe for one of your goals. You can download a template for your marketing recipe at helenharding. co.uk/bonus.

Answer the following questions to create your recipe:

- What is my goal?
- Who is my ideal client?
- What product or service am I offering them?
- What is (are) my marketing recipe(s)?
- Is it working or do I need to change something?

In the following three chapters, I will explore some of the different marketing strategies and activities you can use in more detail.

There are an endless number of options you can employ to market your business so I have outlined some of the popular ones and suggested which type of leads (hot, warm or cold) they are more suitable for. I will not go into too much detail on each as technology is constantly changing, but rather inspire you to work out which are the best fit for you, and to give you some pointers on how to get them up and running.

If you are in the position where you need to find clients quickly, start with the activities that are based on personal connection, focusing on the people who are in your network as you have already built a relationship with them. You will also need to do some of the longer-term activities to build awareness and engage with people who could potentially become your clients in the future. Building awareness is where most practitioners focus their marketing efforts, but these longer-term strategies can leave your appointment book empty in the short term.

Before you do any marketing activity, remember to ask yourself why you are doing it and make sure you have a goal for what you are trying to achieve. There is no point doing something because everyone else is doing it, it has to make sense to you and your business.

TAKEAWAY

Creating a plan and simple recipes will give you the ingredients and steps required to make your vision for your business a reality.

CHAPTER FOURTEEN

Ethical Marketing Activities: Traditional

Personal outreach (hot leads)

Tapping into your personal network is the fastest way to find clients if you need to fill your diary quickly. It is labour intensive because you are connecting with each person individually, but it is the most likely strategy to bring you fast results.

Contact each person on your hot leads list and send them a personalised message (or speak with them) asking for an update, making them an offer, or asking for a referral. It may prompt someone who has been thinking of booking an appointment to actually book one.

You will have people in your network whom you have not worked with and who are not your ideal client, but you can still use this strategy. Instead of appealing to them directly you can use your marketing message to explain whom you help and how you help them. They may know of someone who does need your help which could lead to a referral. This will be the same if you are just starting out, reach out to your personal network asking for referrals. These people already know, like, and trust you, and they will be happy to refer you based on your relationship with them.

Business cards (hot, warm, and cold leads)

Business cards are a powerful tool for your business. They should be part of your basic marketing kit, especially if you are building a local practice. They are a low-cost and portable way to advertise your services and raise your profile. You use them to share your contact information easily and they are a great way to get referrals as other people can share them on your behalf.

Often, a business card is the first impression someone will get of your brand, so you want to make it good. The look and feel of your card will communicate directly to the person receiving it, they will form an opinion on you and the quality of your service, based on it.

Ensure your business cards are consistent with the rest of your branding in terms of colours and fonts. Make use of both sides of your cards by adding your photo and your marketing message. This will help people to remember you, and what you do.

Keep the card as simple as possible and make sure everything on it has a purpose. Information you can use includes:

- Logo
- Name and qualifications
- Your discipline
- Phone number
- Your practice address (if you work from one location)
- Areas covered (if you have several different locations you work from)
- Email address
- Your virtual addresses (website and social media accounts)
- Photograph
- Marketing message

Once you have your content, you need to decide on the size and shape of your business card. An unusual size or shape can make your card stand out; however non-standard formats will add to the production cost.

If you have a graphic designer, brief them to create your artwork so it works with your branding. If you are designing your own, there are templates available online or from printers which you can personalise.

Digital print technology allows you to have small numbers of business cards printed at a low cost. There are endless choices of materials and finishes available from smooth to heavily textured and everything between, white or coloured card, gloss varnished, matt laminated, die-cut, foiled, and embossed to name a few. If you are not used to specifying and ordering print, find examples of cards you like and speak with your local print shop. Alternatively, if you are using an online print service, request a sample of what you are ordering so you can feel the quality and make sure you are happy with them before ordering.

Word of mouth marketing (hot and warm leads)

This marketing strategy requires little budget and is incredibly powerful. Also known as referral marketing, this is one of the oldest marketing strategies and still one of the most effective. Marketing your practice by word of mouth will help you to build a strong foundation of trust around you and your services.

Consider the last time you visited a new restaurant or café recommended by a friend; this is a perfect example of referral marketing in practice. You decided to check out the eatery based on your trust of the person doing the recommending. People naturally trust the opinion of family and friends when they are looking for something new.

Working in health and well-being, you already have a relationship with your clients. You are already close to them because of the nature of your work. Referral marketing means nurturing these existing relationships with a view to attracting new clients.

Your marketing is super focused on those who need your products and services. Your existing clients know exactly how you can help others and will recommend you to the people they know who can benefit too.

There is potential to reach much larger audiences than just family and friends using social media and online reviews. Here technology is amplifying referral marketing. How often do you see people asking for recommendations on social media to solve a problem they have? How often do you look at customer reviews before you buy something on websites? This gives you the potential to reach out to people far beyond your immediate network and the immediate network of your clients, but it relies on your clients sharing their positive experience of working with you.

Building a referral system

Create amazing experiences. Focus on providing your clients with the best possible experience during all their interactions with you. The aim is for them to become a champion of your services and share their amazing results with their peers. The good news of their experience will travel fast and help build your reputation as an expert in your niche. Be aware this will backfire if you are not providing a great experience, so even more reason to go the extra mile and create happy clients.

Exceed expectations. Where appropriate exceed your client's expectations by making life easier for them and showing you care. This could be by providing extra information to support them, checking in by email for an update, giving them a free sample, or sending a handwritten card.

Build relationships. Make an effort to create good relationships with your clients and make them feel special. Show them that you care and that you are interested in them as a person. This personal touch goes a long way to building trust with your clients.

Address issues immediately. The speed and reach of online marketing means you cannot stick your head in the sand and hope a problem will go away of its own accord. You need to address any issues as soon as they are raised to limit any potentially damaging reviews from being posted. You are never going to please everyone, but if you demonstrate respect and fairness people will see through the situation and forgive a lesser review if you handled it well.

Collect testimonials. When a happy client has completed their sessions with you ask for a testimonial. Whether this is an online review on Google or social media or an inspirational client story to share on your website, they are absolute gold for your practice.

Ask for referrals. Depending on your discipline and professional register you may have specific rules around actively asking for referrals. If you are permitted to ask for referrals include this request in your client follow-up process and let clients know you are looking for others just like them whom you can help.

Referral system. Keep yourself on your client's radar and remind them of how helpful you are. This could be something as simple as sending out a monthly newsletter with news, interesting articles, and the opportunity to contact you if they need your help. Create a simple system that helps people refer to you. Make sure it is easy for people to find and contact you. Provide information in different formats which are easy to share across different platforms.

I am in a lucky position where half of my clinical clients come from referrals. This took years to build but has made a world of difference to my practice and helps me avoid the feast and famine cycles. By the time people work with me they already know me and trust that I am the best practitioner for them. I have built up my reputation over the years, but I also put a lot of work into providing helpful marketing and made it easy for people to find me.

Standing out in your local community (warm and cold leads)

It is important to build your profile locally if you want a thriving practice in your community. Being visible within your local area will let people know you exist and connecting with local people will help to build your personal profile.

Make the most of the physical space available both in and around your practice to help you stand out. People are busy and even if they are local, they may not realise you are there. There are things you can do to help grab their attention and inject some personality into your marketing and business too.

Good quality signage

Visible signage is a good marketing tool, reinforcing your brand as well as helping people locate your business. Old and battered signs will affect the perception of the quality of your services and reflect badly on you.

Do not limit signs to a clinic facia, there are many other options available such as nameplates, window graphics, floor graphics, A-frames and notice boards.

Signs do not have to be limited to a clinic; you can have your car branded to help you stand out locally. It will then be a mobile advertisement for your business and go wherever you drive. Depending on your budget and requirements, you can have anything from simple removable magnetic graphics to full vinyl wraps and everything in-between.

Utilising physical space

You can also use your physical space to create word of mouth marketing opportunities as discussed in the previous section. Below are three great examples of how businesses have done this, using items they have available:

- Easygrass, an artificial grass company, covered their cars in artificial grass. A brilliant example of using your physical space to create marketing that people want to talk about and share with their friends.
- Guiseley Osteopaths has "Stan the skeleton" in their clinic window. He has become a bit of a local celebrity. He changes position or is accessorised depending on the season, or current local events. The community love him and share his antics on social media—what a genius idea!
- Whiteboards in some London Underground stations are used to write notes and inspirational poems for customers which they often share on social media—a simple and very effective idea.

Consider what you can do to help you and your practice stand out in the local area. A few suggestions include:

- Paint your front door with a bright and eye-catching colour or paint murals on your walls.
- Create an amazing waiting room which is the ultimate place to relax, or provide extras such as drinks, a children's play corner, or use it as a gallery to display artwork from local artists.
- If you are you known for a certain sense of dress or style, such as wearing a funky hat or a particular colour, embrace it.

Community events

Your local community will have different sorts of events you can get involved in. This could be school fairs, charity events, the Women's Institute, clubs, sports teams, mum and baby groups, summer fairs, craft clubs, community gardens, the list is endless. Ideally, you are looking for communities of people who could be your favourite client. However, all events in your community are worth considering, as it is about building your local profile.

Depending on the type of event, get onto the radar of the organisers by offering your services, or a prize for their competition. Even if you are taking tickets on the door, you can chat to people socially, so they start to get to know your face.

These events are not about selling, they are about raising your profile within your community. You are building your local network as a member of the community by supporting them.

If you identify a support group or club where you can provide help for their members (who are your favourite clients), offer your services and run a talk. If they are not set up for talks, you could create a leaflet or video for their members using your expertise to provide tips. Again, this is not about selling, it is about helping.

Join local online groups where your favourite clients are members. They could focus on their issues, their hobbies and interests, or be about the local community as a whole. Start interacting with people in the group so they get to know you. Most groups have strict guidelines so make sure you stick to the rules. You may find that you can promote things on certain days of the week so take advantage and share your services and events then. The aim is to be super helpful to the members and to make sure they get to know you as a person and experience your support.

Handwritten cards (hot leads)

A simple handwritten card is unexpected in today's online world. Everything is fast, automated and lacks the personal touch you get from receiving an actual envelope through the post. There is something special about receiving a card you can actually hold in your hand and look at.

A card will surprise your client and will mean more than a quick email or text ever will. Because you have taken the time to write to them it shows you care. How would you feel if you received a personal note from someone you respect?

You can send a card for a number of reasons: a thank you note, how are you, saw this and thought of you, the anniversary of their first/last visit to you, basically anything relevant to your relationship with your client. Remember, this is a personal message and not a sales pitch but do include your full name and a way to contact you.

The value comes from the time and thought put into the card and that is what makes all the difference. Just a reminder, for the purpose of data protection, never thank a client for recommending a named person as you will be breaking client confidentiality.

Giving talks (warm and cold leads)

Talks are another great way of marketing your services locally, getting known, and finding new clients. You share your knowledge and build your profile while allowing people to get to know you, experience your style, and understand how you can help them. They are a great way to get started if you want to use public speaking as a marketing strategy for your practice.

If you want to do more speaking, invest time to improve your speaking skills as it will pay dividends and help you grow your confidence. You could start with self-study using videos, books, or online courses. If you want to ramp this up to the next level look into organisations which offer training in public speaking or find a speaking coach to help you hone your art.

Talks provide an opportunity for people to meet you and find out if you are the right person to solve their problems. They will also act as a filter for those who are not a good fit.

Look for opportunities locally where you can share your knowledge such as networking events, clubs in your niche, open days, local shows, exhibitions and health food stores. You could also run your own talks. Find the places where your favourite clients hang out and ask to run a talk there.

Find your presenting style, one that you are comfortable with so you can share your message in a sincere and genuine way. Allow your passion to shine through as you explain how you help people.

Although you are giving the talk, it should focus on answering your audience's questions. You need to provide them with value by educating and entertaining them. You cannot expect to show up and deliver an amazing talk without prior preparation. It takes practice to deliver a talk that works for you and your audience. Your preparation should include:

Goal. Start with your goal for the talk, what do you want to achieve?

Clear message. Have a clear message you want to deliver during the talk. Quality over quantity rules and you do not have to stand and talk for an hour to provide value. Work out the key points you want to get across and create a talk that addresses those without waffling or going into too much detail.

Practise, practise, practise. Even though you know your topic inside out you will still need to practise your talk to get the timing and pace right. It is amazing how much you will change it once you have run through it a few times. A great way to experience your talk is to video yourself and watch it back.

Get your audience involved. The last thing you want is a lot of blank faces staring at you. Have a couple of easy, fun exercises and allow time for a question and answer session.

Be prepared for any objections. Consider any objection people may have so you stay calm and provide appropriate responses if needed.

Next steps. Make sure you finish by explaining clearly and concisely what steps need to be taken so they can work with you.

My regular talk is a very relaxed affair and I do a double act with one of my colleagues. We give a short introduction to the clinic followed by an overview of the key points and then open the floor for questions. It takes around 30 minutes to go through our bit and we allow 30 minutes for questions which gets everyone involved. Our first talks were a whole different story and I cringe thinking about them. We had a presentation packed full of information which took an hour to deliver, let alone allowing time for any questions. Looking back, they were very overwhelming, and we were probably scaring people off! We quickly learnt that keeping our talks simple was a far better option for everyone!

Things do not always go to plan and having a backup is a great way of reducing your stress if things go wrong. If you are using a slide presentation have a printed copy or have your bullet points written on index cards so you are able to confidently give your talk, even if you have a technology meltdown.

Networking (warm and cold leads)

Meeting people in person is a great way to build relationships and get to know potential contacts and clients. Networking is an effective way to meet new clients for many practitioners so it is well worth considering for your marketing activities.

Identify what you want to achieve by attending an event. This could be as simple as meeting an individual who you know is attending or introducing your services to three potential clients.

Today there are many ways to network from paid weekly groups, local meetups, exhibitions, conferences, events, the list goes on but there are a few ways you can ensure you make the most of every opportunity. Do your research on what is available in your area and take into consideration what time commitment you can give to networking as some require you to attend weekly and at the crack of dawn. You also need to discover who the other participants are likely to be as some events are carried out with the same group week in, week out whilst others are industry-based. You want to identify events where your potential clients could be.

Once you have decided the best events to attend, make sure you reflect your brand in terms of how you present yourself including what you wear and the information you distribute, such as leaflets and business cards. Relax, smile, and concentrate on building a warm rapport with people letting your approachable side shine through. Remember, you are there to build relationships and a helpful and engaging manner will put people at ease.

Far too often attendees of networking events are just trying to sell their products and services. I have always found that being interested in other people is a far more successful strategy. By listening and asking great questions you will engage in more useful conversations and in turn people will want to find out more about you.

Once you get back from networking, make sure you follow-up with the people you met. People often go along to meetings and then never get around to following up or leave it too long and the opportunity is lost. If you tell someone that you will drop them an email the following week they will be expecting it, so make sure you follow-up even if it means putting a reminder in your calendar. If you are really organised, make some notes following the meeting so that you have something to refer to when you are sending the email, this will help to personalise it.

Schedule your follow-up a few days after your meeting. That way it is a long enough gap so you do not appear desperate but close enough that they will remember you. Ensure your first email is sent with no strings attached, you do not want to be asking for something at this stage. Instead, see if you can offer them a solution to a problem they mentioned or include a link to an interesting article or research that you think will be of interest to them. If you cannot think of anything specific, a simple "good to meet you and are you going to any other events in the next few months" will suffice, anything to remind them of you and start a conversation.

As with all marketing strategies, make sure you review networking as you may find it is a costly use of your time with little return. A practitioner friend of mine attended a regular weekly meeting for 18 months and she even got involved in running it. Whilst she enjoyed the experience and her profile was raised within the group, the reality was she only gained two clients in all that time as a result of the networking. The cost of attending the meeting every week was four hours of time if you include travel plus the financial cost of getting there, entry, and breakfast. She worked out it cost her over £1,000.00 and 300 hours for two clients, which was not a good return for her time.

Collaborations (hot, warm, and cold leads)

Collaborating with other practitioners is about forming connections to help your business grow. By combining resources and talents, you will be able to offer a broader service to your clients. You may not be able to accomplish something on your own but having two or three people on board can get it done. Here are some of the things to think about if you want to start collaborating with other practitioners:

Have an agreement. Always work out an agreement between you. Decide how things will work, who is responsible for what, and how you will split any profits you make. Deciding these in advance will stop any awkward conversations later on.

Inspiration. Spending hours researching on your own for inspiration for your business and marketing is not always enough. You will get to a point where you cannot see the woods for the trees. It is the sharing of ideas and bouncing them around with others that inspires creativity, gives different perspectives and identifies opportunities.

Grow your network. Being a successful practitioner requires you to continuously build and nurture your network. You need to regularly meet new people in order to keep bringing clients to your door. Finding new people to connect with, even if you do not end up collaborating with them will build your network and raise your profile.

Self-awareness. Whilst most practitioners wear every hat in their business, there are some tasks they should not do. Collaborating with others forces you to recognise and admit your strengths and weaknesses. This will help you to allocate tasks to the best person for the job rather than trying to do everything yourself.

Save money. If you are splitting the costs of a project or marketing activities with another practitioner you will either save money or double your budget. For example, sharing a stand at an exhibition with a collaborator means both of you share the cost of the stand. Both of you market to your own audience to increase the number of visitors and the number of potential clients being introduced to your practice.

Not every collaboration will work. Sometimes it takes working with someone to find out you are not a good fit. Learn from the experience and you will be prepared next time an opportunity presents itself.

Recently, a friend who is a Pilates teacher has been working with a medical herbalist to run workshops locally on joint health. They have a similar client group but work in very different ways which complement each other. By creating a joint workshop they split the work and associated costs whilst still growing their individual businesses.

Practice leaflet (cold leads)

A leaflet can be a great marketing opportunity if you do it right. Technology has brought the price of creating and printing one right down, making them a cost-effective form of marketing your practice. There are, however, a few things to avoid when designing a leaflet:

Making the leaflet all about you. Clients do want to know about you, but it has to start with them. Having you at the front and centre of your leaflet will put people off in the first place, unless they are specifically looking for you.

Having your logo as the main feature on the front cover. Whilst your brand or name is important to you it is not the first thing a potential client is looking for and will not mean anything unless you already have a local profile.

Making it all about your discipline. People often do not understand or know which discipline will help them, they are looking for a solution to their problem.

Bad design. Consider using a designer to create your leaflet so it looks professional. If you do not have the budget use a simple template and keep the overall look (colours, photos, fonts) in line with your brand. This way, if someone checks out your website after seeing your leaflet there is a common look and feel to it.

Bad copy. Again, this is where it pays to keep things simple, from the message you are sharing to the language you use. Get a friend to proof-read your copy to make sure it makes sense and there are no glaring errors. Break up big blocks of copy to make it easier to read and more interesting to the eye.

General leaflets. The temptation to create a leaflet that covers lots of different issues may appear like a good idea, but it is unlikely to be effective. In general, people are looking for a specific solution to their problems.

How to create a leaflet that works

This is where the advantage of having a niche comes into its own. Being able to describe who your client is and how you can help them is price-less. The ability to target your marketing to specific people will help you to attract their attention.

Be helpful. Create a leaflet that advertises your expertise but do it in a way that demonstrates that you understand the issues around it, what drives people to look for your help and what their concerns are. Imagine someone has trouble sleeping and they are faced with a plethora of leaflets competing for their attention. Are they likely to pick the one titled "Hypnotherapy" or are they going to pick the one titled "How to improve your sleep naturally"?

Introduce your services. While the aim of the leaflet is to provide information, make sure you keep space to introduce yourself too. Write a short bio including a photo and brief details of how you work. Include the type of results your clients achieve and a testimonial.

Tell them their next step. Tell people how they can work with you and include your contact details.

Public relations (cold leads)

Public relations (PR) is a great option as it is effectively free advertising and if you do your own PR the only cost is your time. PR done well will provide you with credibility and help to build trust in your brand.

The world of media is changing fast. A few years ago, when you tried to get PR for your practice it was about getting featured in newspapers, magazines, and on radio or TV. Being featured in the traditional press is still a powerful marketing strategy but there are a host of other media opportunities which include blogs, online magazines, video channels, social media, and podcasts to name a few. Businesses are becoming their own media companies. You can become one yourself or share your stories with other aligned media platforms.

If you decide to use PR as a way of marketing your business, here are a few considerations to get you started.

Have your house in order. Before you start doing anything, make sure your own website and social media profiles are all up to date. With any PR, the journalist or media owner will want to check you out and you want to give a good and consistent impression.

Know your message. You can comment on anything where you have an opinion or experience, even if it is not directly related to your business it will help to raise your profile. You have a list of the topics you can speak about from Chapter 6, Creating your personal brand so use these as inspiration and to ensure there is consistency in what you share.

You will need to be able to clearly articulate what you do in your business so use your marketing message from Chapter 10, Marketing basics.

Do your research. Spend time researching the publications and content your favourite client consumes. What magazines or websites do they read? What videos or podcasts do they subscribe to? Do they listen to the radio or watch TV?

Make a list of your client's favourites and decide which you are interested in getting featured in. Buy copies, watch or read the content they produce and get to know them and the type of stories they share. Find out about the schedules they work to as many, especially traditional media, are planned and compiled months ahead of publication.

Invest time in creating relationships. Find out who writes or creates the media and follow them on social media. Journalists are known for spending time on Twitter and sending out requests for articles they are writing. Get on a journalist's radar by being helpful, sharing their information, commenting, and basically connecting with them. Then, when you decide to send them an email pitching a story they will have some idea of who you are. When you do get published, make sure you show your appreciation and share their content with your audiences.

What is the story? Whilst you want to raise awareness of your business, getting featured in the media is not all about you. Journalists and media contacts are busy people and they want to know the benefit to them. They want stories that are different, and that their audience will want to know about, and will connect with. Why is it important for their people to know about your story?

Keep your pitch simple. Rather than trying to be clever, keep your pitch to the journalist or media owner clear and simple. Do not make them work hard to understand the story you are sharing as it will have the opposite effect and be deleted. Instead, give them the necessary information in a few lines and demonstrate why you are a good fit for their audience.

Results require consistency. As with all marketing, PR is a game of consistency and getting featured once is not enough to have clients flooding through your door. You need to see it as a marathon and not a sprint and consistently find ways of being featured.

RECOMMENDED READING: *Your Press Release is Breaking My Heart* **by Janet Murray**

Janet is a former journalist and walks you through the process of getting press coverage for your business. Having spent years being bombarded by terrible pitches, she took on the challenge of teaching small businesses how to stand out in a sea of bland pitches and to get their story noticed.

Setting up a stand (cold leads)

A stand is a great way to build your profile locally and introduce your services to potential clients. It can be very low cost and because you are on the stand you get to meet and talk to lots of people, it can be a brilliant way to market your services and get known.

You need permission to set up a stand. Look out for where other small businesses and organisations have stands and approach the venue to find out how you can book a stand there too. For example, local shows, artisan markets, craft fairs, open days, and conferences all offer good opportunities. Look for anywhere your favourite clients are likely to be and go there.

One of my clients recently discovered that a big supermarket likes to support local small businesses. She was able to secure a stand in the entrance lobby where she could chat with people and invite them along to a talk she was doing locally.

Making your stand, stand out

When you are in a busy environment you need to make your stand visible to attract attention. Try and find out where your stand will be and what is provided by the venue. This way you can ensure you bring along anything else you need.

A plain table can be easily dressed using a tablecloth (a single sheet or throw will also work just as well) in your brand colours. Add height and interest with items that have relevance to your discipline. If you have the time and budget have pull-up roller banners created, you will be able to use these over and over again. If not, look at what you have available and be creative using plants, displays of products, and models, basically anything that will catch people's attention and initiate a conversation.

As you are manning your stand and marketing your services, remember you are your brand. Wear something that makes you feel good, fits with your colours and branding, and the sort of item you wear for work. There is absolutely no point wearing a suit if you never wear one while you work.

Make sure the information you give to people includes how they can contact you. Business cards are a good option but consider creating leaf-lets including useful tips for your ideal clients which are valuable for your visitors to keep.

Have a way of collecting people's contact details to either get back to them with the requested information and/or add them to your email list (with permission). This can be as simple as having a notebook, create an email sign-up form or have a smartphone or tablet where people can sign-up directly for your emails.

As you will be available to talk, those already in your audience may want to come and meet you too. Share where you will be on social media and talk about it locally to help spread the word.

TAKEAWAY

Do not underestimate the power of traditional marketing activities. Many of them are still the fastest way to attract clients to your practice.

CHAPTER FIFTEEN

Ethical Marketing Activities: Website

Website (hot, warm, and cold leads)

The first place we generally turn to when researching new things is the internet. Your decision to work with someone will be influenced by their website and how easily you find what you are looking for.

When new practitioners think of marketing, they often think of a website. Whilst a website does provide you with an online home, it is a huge project and should not automatically be top of your priority list, especially when you are starting out. There are other things you can do to cultivate an online presence until you are in the position to start building your own website, for example claim your Google My Business page, create social media pages, and add your details to relevant online directories. More on these in the next chapter.

This does not mean you should not build a website; professional marketers agree having an online presence is a necessity these days. You will need one if you are serious about building a business bigger than your personal practice. A website will provide you with other options for creating different income streams, but it should not come above finding clients for your business and bringing in income.

Building a website from scratch is a big job and do not underestimate how much time it takes to write copy and pull all the information together. There are lots of options for creating a website which can feel overwhelming at first. Whilst technology and styles change constantly, there are some basic steps you can take to help you create yours.

Recognise that your website will be a never-ending project, constantly requiring updating and nurturing to get the most from it. A website is not a static "brochure" which is finished once you go live, it will need regular updates in terms of content and as technology changes upgrades may be necessary as well; be aware of the commitment you are taking on before you start. If you do create a website and do nothing with it, it will not fulfil its potential as a marketing tool. Search engines such as Google like fresh, current content to deliver to their customers and if yours does not get updated regularly it will not appear as relevant to them and may not appear in searches.

There are many different options to build a website:

Templated system. There are some amazing templated systems available which will help you create a professional-looking website. If you pay for a package you will have access to support if any difficulties arise. If you decide to use one of the free systems and come up against issues you may struggle to get the help you require.

Design your own. You can learn how to design your own website. This will be a huge learning curve and certainly not an undertaking for anyone who is technically challenged. You will not have support if things go wrong and will have to figure things out for yourself, but it is totally possible with the technology we have available today.

Professionally built from a template. A professional developer will make sure you have a beautiful website, but they will use a templated system to create it, saving you a lot of money compared to having one designed specifically for you.

Bespoke design. This is the premium option if you can afford it and prices will vary dramatically depending on what you want your website to do and how complicated it is. If a professional designs your website, they will make sure the design reflects you perfectly, it does everything you want, and is fully functioning. You will be able to arrange ongoing support to keep it updated and working properly.

If you decide to employ someone to build your website, make sure you know how to make simple changes to it yourself. I have seen many practitioners spend a lot of money having a beautiful website created and then they have to pay someone every time they want to upload a blog post or change copy. Your website will continuously evolve, it is important for you to be able to make amendments and add content to it, or it could get very expensive.

Start simply

Decide what you need your website to do, to support your business now. There will always be ways you can develop it going forward, but if you need to get an online presence quickly, start simply. A fully functioning website can take months to put together and some practitioners will procrastinate over theirs for years. At the end of the day, you work in health and well-being and although a website is your online home you are not expected to have a big flashy one that does everything apart from making the tea. Start with one that has the minimum functions required to do a good job and no more.

Think about the way a visitor will want to use your website. Your website is not for you, it is for your clients and you want them to have a great experience and to be able to find what they are looking for.

Spend time looking at other websites and create a reference file of things you love and the things you hate about other websites. Do not limit yourself to looking at websites in health and well-being as you will be able to learn a lot from different types of business. Look at how easy they are to navigate and the design of them, how do they make you feel? Once you have done your research think about the things that are important to include on your website:

- What must it have?
- What should it have?
- What could it have? These are things you can add later so they are not needed now.
- What will it absolutely not have?

Go low-tech and get a big sheet of paper and some coloured pens. Start planning out how you want your website to be used by your clients. Think about creating a roadmap that takes them on the minimum journey possible to get to a decision, whether that is to book a discovery call with you or to book into a workshop. You do not need an all-singing, all-dancing website at this stage, your website just needs to be user-friendly and show clients the way.

Then consider the design of your website and how it will look with your branding and photographs. If you are briefing a designer to create your website, they will want to understand your likes and dislikes as well as what you want your website to do. They will take the information you provide and turn it into a website that represents you and your practice. If you are doing your own website keep it simple and work with the template you have chosen, you will have to compromise in some places but it is better to have a simple website that is clear than one that is messy and cluttered. Keep the number of colours and fonts to a minimum too, if you use too many it will make your website look amateur.

Refresh your existing website

If you already have a website and feel it is not working, it may be able to get away with a refresh rather than going to the expense of creating a new one. Start by reviewing your existing website, it may just need to be given the opportunity to perform. If, however, it is very old, broken, or does not work with modern technology you will need to get a new site.

- Does your website clearly demonstrate whom you help, how you help them and the results they can expect to achieve?
- Does it look professional and reflect you and your brand?
- Is it simple to navigate for visitors who are researching your services?
- How well is your copy written and what tone of voice does it have?
- Ask for feedback on your website from people who represent your niche and could be your client. It is also useful to get feedback from someone who understands websites and marketing.

Map out your website and how you want it to work in the same way you would if you were starting from scratch with a new website (see the previous section). Work out what you already have in place and what updates are needed to make the most of the website you already have.

Prioritise the list of updates according to the must have, should have, could have, and absolutely not categories. Cross off anything that falls into the "absolutely not" category. You now have a list to work to which you can split into the things you can do and those you need help with. Now start to work your way through the list, doing one job at a time, and before you know it your website will be updated.

Remember, your website will always be work in progress and will never be perfect, but you do not always need the expense of a new one to make it work for you.

About page

The "About" page is one of the most viewed pages on a website and it is where your reader has the opportunity to connect with you through your personal story. It provides an insight into who you are, your personality, why you do what you do, and more importantly, why they would want to work with you.

There are a lot of opinions around what you should include on the "About" page of your website and there is no one right, or perfect answer. Here are some pointers for how to write your "About" page:

Research other "about" pages. Get an idea of what you do and do not like as this will provide inspiration when you are creating yours. Think about what really resonates with you and the details that draw you into that person's life and experiences, from the length of the page to how much information is being shared.

Inspiration. Collect your ideas together from the work you did in Chapter 4 on Your why and in Chapter 6 on Your story. It will help you to communicate what makes you unique, your skills, and qualities. Write your story and decide how you want visitors to feel about it when they read your page.

Write in the first person. Make sure you write in the way you communicate naturally and that the style and the tone reflect you.

Add images and videos. As a minimum, include a profile photo, people want to see the real you especially if they are planning on working with you. Include a video where you are explaining something relevant to your clients, if you have one. Video is completely under-utilised by many practitioners and a brilliant way of standing out. This was something I avoided for ages, but once I posted a video I was pleasantly surprised by how many people commented on it and said that it influenced their decision to choose me as their practitioner.

Professional qualifications. Include any which support your experience and passion as a practitioner but do not include your full

CV and every qualification you have, especially if it brings nothing to the party.

Logos. Add in any logos from qualifications, professional bodies, or where you have appeared in the press or other PR as they will provide evidence of your credibility if they are appropriate to your business.

Connect. This is the perfect place to include other ways for your viewer to connect with you, include your email sign-up form and any links to social media.

Although it is your "About" page, it is not all about you! Remember that everything on your website is ultimately about what you can do for the reader and your "About" page is no different. A visitor to this page will want to know what is in it for them so start with a statement which makes it clear to the reader that they are in the right place. Use the body of the text to introduce yourself, describe your journey, and relay why you do what you do.

Show your softer side and include information you feel comfortable sharing and is appropriate for your audience with a few details of your home life or hobbies. By knowing that you are a mum, or that you support a certain charity, or have a particular interest or hobby will help the readers get to know you as a person. You could include a quirky little-known fact about yourself, or something that makes you laugh, it does not have delve into the depths of your personal life but just provide a little insight into your personality and what makes you tick.

Search engine optimisation

In its simplest terms, search engine optimisation (SEO) are the activities you do to help your website get picked up in relevant online searches. It will be based on what people are asking for and how relevant and authoritative Google thinks your website is.

Think about the service Google is providing to their users. They want to provide the best and most relevant information to answer the questions being asked of it. The better the match your website is to the question asked, the more likely you will show up in someone's search.

Keywords are the words and phrases that people are typing into Google to find you. Think about the last thing you typed into Google; you will have asked it a very specific question based on what you were searching for. It is the specific questions your favourite client is looking to answer that you want to include on your website. As well as finding the right keywords and phrases, the quality of your website, how well it is maintained, and how secure it is will affect its findability.

Ultimately, the content you write on your website is for your audience and not for Google. Be mindful of SEO but do not spend all your time manipulating your copy to fit in keywords. It is far better to have an easy to read website that is designed to help the reader than a clunky one that does not flow. Going into any detail on SEO is outside of my area of expertise and the remit of this book but it is something you need to be aware of when setting up your website.

Marketing your website

You may have the best website in the world but if you do not market it you will make it difficult for people to find it. You need to find ways of sharing your website with your potential clients and encourage them to visit it. In addition to doing your SEO, you can do a lot of other activities to promote your website and attract visitors to it.

Other options for promoting your website are:

- Include links to your website on your personal social media profiles. That way family and friends will be able to check out your information and recommend you to others
- Build professional pages on social media platforms and share your content and thoughts
- Send updates out to your email list with links to your posts
- Participate in social media group discussions and share links to your information and website in relevant conversations. Make sure you abide by the group rules though
- Put a link to your website in your email signature
- Include your website address on any business cards, flyers, or posters you create
- List your services in relevant online directories with links to your website
- Write guest blog posts for other websites and get links back to yours
- Be interviewed on podcasts, videos, or live broadcasts
- Have car graphics that include your website address

Content creation (hot, warm, and cold leads)

You could argue that everything you do in marketing is creating content of some description. However, I am talking specifically about the content created for your website which can then be shared on other platforms. The main types of content created are written, graphics, audio, and video.

Focus on producing one core type of content which can then be repurposed in other ways. Pick one that suits your strengths and you enjoy doing as you are much more likely to be consistent with it.

Blogging

If writing is your strength, blogging is a great option for you. If you are just starting with content marketing, it is also one of the least technically demanding ways of adding content to your website. Writing posts can help you build your confidence, especially if you are nervous about recording your voice or putting yourself on camera.

Writing articles allows you to demonstrate your knowledge and is a versatile way of creating content. They can be short and to the point, provide step-by-step instructions, or you can go in-depth on a topic.

You can add interest to your blog posts by using images and graphics to illustrate and support the topic. This will help to break up the copy, make it more visually appealing, and you can then use them to promote your article on social media.

Creating written content is very important for your website as tells search engines what is on the page. Even if you create other types of content such as podcasts, infographics, or videos, they will need copy to accompany them, even if it is a simple summary of the content.

If you decide you want to start blogging, you will find useful tips in Chapter 17, Marketing lessons.

Infographics

"A picture is worth a thousand words" according to the English adage. If you love creating artwork, infographics are a visual way of sharing information clearly and quickly. Use them to share knowledge, data, tips, and step-by-step instructions in a way that is engaging and interesting.

If you do not have the technology yourself, there are plenty of free online software options available to help you create professional-looking infographics. They are great to use on your website but also brilliant to share on social media as they are visually appealing and will attract engagement.

If you want to start creating your own infographics, start by researching others to decide which ones you feel work the best, and what styles you like. Collate a few examples for reference and to inspire your own design. Gather the information you want to convey and sketch out the graphic, using images and symbols to get the message across with the least amount of words possible. It will force you to be concise with your copy as you need to communicate the idea visually without an overwhelming number of words.

You can then create your own infographic, or for best results send your brief to a graphic designer. Whoever produces the artwork, keep the design of the graphics in line with your brand guidelines so there is a recognisable look and feel to them.

Podcasting

If you love talking, podcasts are a great way to create content and connect with your audience. Podcasts are popular as listeners can literally consume them on the go whether that is walking the dog, at the gym, or driving the car. There is no limit to the length of a show, and they can vary between a few minutes to over an hour.

When you listen to a podcast regularly, you feel like you know the host personally. You start to build a relationship with them and have a sense of who they are and what they stand for. This is what makes them such a powerful marketing strategy for practitioners.

I created a series of 50 podcasts with a colleague when they first started to become popular a few years ago. Listening to them today, I cringe! They now feel dated and a little amateur because we did not really know what we were doing when we started. We wrote, recorded, and edited them ourselves. But they continue to attract clients, years after they were produced and provide value to our clients. When clients are researching our training, they listen to them and get to know us and our style so when it comes to picking a practitioner, we are the first choice because they already know us.

Podcasts are reasonably easy to record and edit, but you can outsource the editing if you have the budget. Podcasts are free to create if you do them yourself, and if you do not already have any software you can download free options online for editing and recording. The software providers include tutorials to walk you through getting started which is a great help and will have you recording in no time.

You may need some assistance from your web developer to link everything up properly but once the system is set up it will be easy to maintain.

Video

It is estimated by 2022 82 per cent of all internet traffic will be video-based (Cisco.com). Video is becoming increasingly important for anyone who wants to improve their presence online and is the first choice of media for many online marketers.

Video is the best way for people to really get a sense of who you are and your style. It is also one of the least utilised versions of content created by practitioners. You can really stand out from the crowd if you produce videos. I certainly recommend you have at least one video on your website introducing yourself and your services.

Create helpful videos for your clients and potential clients in the form of a vlog. Vlogging has become increasingly popular with people earning a living from producing their own video shows. Vlogs do not have to be super polished, but they have to provide value and you need to be consistent in producing them. There is the option to create live video on social media and save them to use as a vlog later.

The second biggest search engine is YouTube, which is owned by Google. Having your own YouTube channel and creating videos will increase your chances of being found online.

Technology has advanced and you can create a great quality video using your phone. You can improve the quality by shooting in natural daylight, simply stand in front of a window with the camera between you and the window. Do not get stuck thinking you need lots of equipment, just start with what you have available.

Plan out what you want to talk about and then create simple videos which are a few minutes long sharing your thoughts and tips with the camera. If you hate the idea of putting yourself on camera, you can create videos by recording a presentation, a carousel of photos, or creating an animation which you can narrate. Add captions to your videos so if someone is watching without sound, they can follow you. These can be done as you record with some software or added later. Once recorded, keep any editing as simple as possible and do what you can on your phone.

When you are happy with your video, upload it to YouTube or another video hosting service and then embed it on your website, the video will then appear on your page. Never save a video directly to your website as the files are large and it will slow your website down.

RECOMMENDED READING: *Vlog Like a Boss* by Amy Shmittauer

Amy is a successful vlogger and walks you through the process of creating a vlog and deals with the fears that stop people publishing.

TAKEAWAY

Your website is your online home and has the potential to be an amazing asset for your business. Start simply and develop it as your practice grows.

CHAPTER SIXTEEN

Ethical Marketing Activities: Online

Email list (hot and warm leads)

It is never too early to start building your email list and it is an asset for your business. The value of an email list is it allows you to contact people directly with their permission. It does not have to be complicated or hard work and the rewards to your business can be huge. Online marketers put a lot of work into building their email list as it is the number one way most of them make sales.

You need to have explicit permission to send people emails otherwise they are considered to be spam and are against data protection legislation. People on your list have the right to unsubscribe, withdrawing their permission for you to email them so you need a way of keeping track of this. The simplest way to do this is to use an email service provider as they will manage this for you. There are many different free plans available and for most practitioners these are a great starting point.

You will find the main email service providers are keen to sign you up and will make it easy for you to get started by providing tutorials and templates. They will manage your list for you and new subscribers can automatically be added from your website. Alternatively, you can import lists you already have or you can add in people manually. The service will also automatically remove anyone who unsubscribes making sure your email marketing observes the legal requirements. They provide you with analytics so you will know how many people join your list, how many of your emails are opened and as you send more, you will be able to tell which topics are most appealing to your clients.

The following is a quick overview of where to start with email marketing:

Set up an account with an email service provider. If you only want to start with sending out updates or a newsletter keep it simple by starting with a free account. If you want to do more advanced email marketing such as setting up automated email sequences, this will require a paid service.

Website form. You may want to ask your website developer for help with this. Your website is an ideal place for people to sign-up to your email list. If you entice people with a gift for example a free guide or a meditation download, they have to give you separate permission to receive regular emails.

Invite existing clients. Send a personal email to your existing clients asking if they would like to join your list. Make sure you describe the benefits of joining and keep it simple by saying something like "reply to this email with 'sign me up' and I will do it for you". If you make it easy for people they are more likely to say yes.

Email your network. Send a personal email to people in your network of friends, family, and colleagues to let them know what you are doing. Ask if they would like to be added to your list (if they are in your niche) and/or whether they would pass your details onto anyone they know who may benefit from your services.

Social media. Post on your social media accounts letting friends and contacts know about your services and how they can sign-up to your list.

Email sign-up form. Create a paper version of your sign-up form so you have one ready to use when you are networking or working with clients.

Re-engage an old email list. All is not lost if you have a list you started but have not used it. Take the opportunity to re-ignite it by sending an honest email acknowledging your lack of contact, then whet their appetite by announcing that you are going to be sending out some exciting new information in the coming months. You can remind them they can unsubscribe if they no longer wish to hear from you. I had to do this following a particularly challenging few months when I did not email my list. I hated admitting how slack I had been (especially as I should know better!), but I put my big girl pants on and used the subject line "Life Threw me Lemons". It was amazing how receptive people were to hearing back from me and how many supportive replies I received. Yes, I got a few unsubscribes, but they were never going to be my clients so that was fine.

Once you have started collecting people onto your email list you need to start sending out emails consistently. There is no point in building a list if it just sits there, doing nothing. This is your starting point and there are lots of more advanced things you can do with email but start simple and start building your list sooner rather than later.

Email newsletter (hot and warm leads)

Email newsletters are an inexpensive way of marketing your services, costing little more than your time so is a perfect option for practitioners. It is one of the main marketing activities which helped me to grow my practice and I get appointments off the back of mine every month.

Use an email provider. Do not try and do this from your work email account. Create your newsletter with an email service provider as described in the previous section.

Timing. For newsletters to work well they need to be sent out regularly. Work out what is achievable for you, within your current schedule, and commit to that. If you can only do one a month that is fine, it is better to commit to that rather than trying to do one a week and lasting two weeks before you miss one.

Content. Keep the content of your newsletter simple and create a basic template you can use each time you produce it. It does not have to be flashy or very long, it is simply about providing value to your client and reminding them you are there.

Three key elements to include in your newsletter are:

- Personal update, allow your readers to peek into your world and allow them to relate to you on a personal level
- Main article including useful information demonstrating your expertise in the area
- Make an offer of some description, such as booking a discovery call or attending your workshop

You can also include other elements to add interest including:

- Inspirational quotes
- News from your practice
- Links to your recent blog posts
- Recommended reading or resources
- Images
- Testimonials
- Meal plans and recipes
- Exercises

Writing your newsletter. Copywriting basics are covered in more detail in Chapter 17, Marketing lessons. In general, make your newsletter chatty and write using the same language you would use when speaking. The introduction is where your reader can get to know you and you can share stories or updates. Depending on your chosen topic write in a style to reflect the content and avoid any jargon, keeping your language simple.

Layout and design. Decide if you want to reflect your brand in your newsletter or keep it looking like a simple email. Most email providers provide pre-designed templates you can use, or you can create your own. Once you have set up your first newsletter you can simply copy it and change the content for the next issue.

Social media (hot, warm, and cold leads)

Social media is here to stay and love it or hate it, it is an effective way of marketing your local practice as well as building a local audience. It is a constantly changing environment and can be overwhelming so when starting out with your business keep it really simple.

Social media platforms want to provide their users with the best experience and they use algorithms to work out what to deliver to them based on what is popular and engaging. Engagement will affect how many people your posts are shown to.

Here are a few ways to make the most of social media for your practice:

Focus your efforts. When starting out, focus on one platform and get really good with that before branching out onto others. If you are not familiar with a new platform spend time getting to know it and understand how it works and how people interact there. Your choice of platform also needs to be where your favourite clients are, there is no point marketing yourself somewhere they will not see you.

Consistency. Getting a following on social media is a long-term strategy, it takes work and you have to be consistent to get results from it. When you start out, it will help you to get the support of family and friends and ask them to comment on and like your posts. This will help the algorithms understand you produce content that is interesting which will help them get shown to more people.

Build your email list. Avoid building your whole business on a social media platform as you are in effect building your online home on rented land. If the rules change, you have no control and could suddenly find your page or profile removed and you are left with no way of contacting your connections. Make sure you also build your email list so you can contact people directly should the worse happen.

Consistent brand and message. When you set up your page or profile, make sure it fits with your brand and that you include a photo of yourself. People want to connect with other humans, and you are using social media to raise awareness and engage with people. Ensure your information makes it clear whom you help but also gives a sense of you as a person. Avoid being too generic, your page or profile should not be interchangeable with any other practitioner in a similar discipline, with only your name to differentiate you!

Have a plan. Decide what you are trying to achieve from the platform, so you have a plan of action rather than just chucking information out there. What is the point of the information you are sharing? Everything you do should inspire, educate, or entertain your audience and you want to post things people want to see. Having your list of topics you post on (chapter 6, Creating your personal brand), will help you decide what is right for you to share. I look at creating an editorial calendar in the next chapter which will help you with this.

Start conversations. Remember people do not want to have conversations with brands, they want to speak with other humans. Whatever you do, do not connect with someone and then try to sell to them immediately as this will have the opposite effect. Be social and be helpful. Find others with similar audiences to you and start to comment and like the information they are sharing.

Respond to comments. If someone spends time and energy commenting on your posts make sure you respond to them. It will make them feel valued and help you to build a connection with them.

Google My Business Page (cold leads)

If you run a practice where you see clients in person you qualify for a free Google My Business (GMB) page. You can increase your online presence by setting up a GMB page even if you do not have a website. GMB allows you to manage how you appear in Google searches and maps. The pages allow Google to provide answers to its users in one place without having to go off and visit different websites, so make sure you are listed.

Your page includes general information about your business, photos, promotions and you can also collect reviews and respond to them. Ask happy clients to leave a review on your GMB page as it provides evidence of the quality of your work. If you do happen to receive a negative review it is important to respond to it and address it in a professional and courteous way as these reviews are public and you want to leave a good impression at all costs.

Online directories (cold leads)

There are numerous online directories, many of which are free to use. They can provide valuable opportunities for you to list your details for very little effort.

Online directories and lists can be set up by individuals, professional bodies, or companies and can be free or paid for. Some directories will be completely out of date and not maintained in any obvious way. Avoid these as they are going to be a waste of your time and energy. Others may already list you even if you have not submitted your details. Google your name and see where it appears online. Make sure you claim the directory listings for yourself so potential clients read what you want them to about you and your services.

Any directories that are managed by professional bodies will have certain requirements for you to be listed. This could include being a member for which there will probably be a cost associated and certain levels of education, qualifications, and/or experience. It is certainly worth joining the directories of any professional bodies that you are already a member of. If you are joining one as a new member check out the advantages of becoming a member and the potential hoops you may need to jump through, it needs to be worth your time and money to join.

When looking for the best directories to list your business in, search online for your profession plus directory, for example "osteopath directory" and see which ones come up the highest in the search results, these should be the ones with the most traffic. Review them to see if they look professional, feel like a good fit for your business, and will reflect you accurately.

Another trick to finding directories is to Google the names of other practitioners in your local area to see where they are listed. It is useful to appear in the same places, especially if they are free listings.

If you are considering a paid service, you need to make sure that you get a good return on your investment. What benefits are you going to get from handing over your hard-earned cash? Does this directory have access to the type of client that you want to work with? Is it focused on your particular discipline or is it a more general one?

Whilst there is a huge benefit from having links to your website and contact details for your business, it is best to make sure they are accurate, that the work required getting them in place is focused and they are going to benefit your practice.

You should review any listings you have on a regular basis, especially the paid ones, to check they are still working for you. If they are not paying for themselves and generating enquiries make sure they are not renewed automatically, you do not want to pay for a listing that does not send you clients.

Online advertising (cold leads)

Have you been thinking about advertising your health and well-being business with paid online advertising? If this is one of your chosen marketing strategies it needs to be done strategically to make the most of your money. Getting paid advertising wrong can cost you dearly.

With all paid advertising, professional help to get advertisements (ads) set up properly is a good investment. You can pay someone to do them on your behalf or do a course to understand how to set the ads up properly for yourself. You will also have to allow enough of a budget to test out what works and what does not.

Google ads. Depending on your discipline and the services you offer, Google Ads is often a good option, especially if you work with very personal issues. If you think about it, most people turn to Google first for a solution to their problems, even nicknaming it "Dr Google".

Many of my practitioner colleagues have taken out paid ads on Google very successfully.

You need to understand how keywords (the phrases people type into the search box on Google) work. There will be an amount of trial and error even if you use professional services to create your ads. If you decide to go solo and set up your own Google Ads campaign there are comprehensive step-by-step videos and checklists available from Google. Simply search for "Setting up Google Ads" to find the latest version. You definitely need to invest time in understanding them before spending any money.

Social media ads. These are another popular option but again you need to be strategic in how you go about these. People are on social media to be sociable rather than looking for solutions to their problems. They may not want people knowing that they are struggling so may be less likely to engage if it could be seen by a friend. I would query if promoting services around sensitive issues is a good fit on social media, perhaps Google may be a better option. There are strict restrictions on what you can advertise, especially in relation to health and well-being. Check the guidelines on the platform before spending any time creating ads, you do not want to run the risk of having them blocked.

There are creative ways you can use ads on social media which will work well for practitioners. These ads are designed to build connections and relationships with your audience. Gone are the days where blasting out messages like "buy my thing" connects with anyone. These ads just get lost in the sea of information we are bombarded with continuously. How often do you buy something directly from an ad you see in your newsfeed? People need to see messages numerous times before they are likely to entertain them. If you are selling a health and well-being service the number of times increases. People need to get to know who you are and what you stand for before they decide you are the right person for them. Because of this, you are better off using social media ads to position yourself as someone who is helpful. This is aimed at building relationships and connection. Potential clients will start to get to know you and to trust you so they are confident to take the next steps with you when they are ready. This way of using ads is a long-term strategy and about building relationships rather than a quick fix.

There is an art to paid ads whichever platform you decide to use, and you will have to invest time and money testing your ads until you discover what does and does not work. If you have the budget there are agencies that can help you work out the best strategy and set up your ads. They will speed up the whole process, but it will still take a period of time to really understand what works so be prepared for this. If you do not have the budget, you can do a course to learn how to use different ad systems which will help you make the most of your money.

TAKEAWAY

Online marketing is a great way to build your local practice as well as providing an opportunity to reach a global audience.

CHAPTER SEVENTEEN

Marketing Lessons

When you are marketing yourself there is so much to learn. It can be overwhelming trying to work out the best way of doing things so here are a few basic lessons which will help you make the most of your time and budget.

Copywriting basics

Many practitioners suffer from writing demons and struggle to write, or even to decide what they should write about. I would love to tell you it is easy and your first attempts will be amazing, but I would be lying (unless you are a naturally gifted writer). I spent years believing I could not write and had nothing to say that was interesting, and now here I am writing a book! My first job was in a design studio and I was surrounded by amazing writers and proof-readers and was often the butt of jokes over my inability to spell or use grammar correctly. My inner perfectionist created the belief that I could not write, and this kept me hiding for years and avoiding doing anything that involved writing in any way. I had to do a lot of work on myself to build my confidence and get started.

Anyone who has been writing for a while and reviews their early work will be embarrassed by it and you will be no different. You will get better with practice and like any new skill you must put the work in to learn. The more you do, the easier it will be and the faster you will get. I may not be the most accomplished writer but I have written hundreds of articles and now a book, I am happy I took the plunge and got started. If I can do it, so can you!

Unfortunately, most practitioners do not have the budget to hire a professional copywriter, so it is up to you to create the copy for your business. Learning to write copy will really help you with your marketing whether it is for your website, social media posts, or writing articles. You are the best person to communicate your passion so writing is a skill worth investing your time in as it will pay dividends in the long run. Below are useful lessons that I have picked up along my journey which I think will be helpful for you:

Create templates. Especially for the things you write regularly as it will save you a huge amount of time. You will find they vary depending on what you are writing. Your blog post template will be different from your newsletter template. Having these means you can literally fill in the relevant information and your piece will start to take shape quickly.

A typical blog post template could include:

- Title
- Short introduction
- Sections with subheadings each covering a point, example, or tip
- Summary
- Next step, what do you want the reader to do next?
- Inspirational quote for social media artwork
- Links to relevant information such as blogs, videos, and podcasts

Make it personal. Imagine your favourite client is reading your piece and write directly to them as if you are having a conversation. Keep your writing in the first person using I, you, we, and me, rather than in the third person which can make you feel distant and unfriendly. Keep your language simple and avoid big or technical words which will only confuse the reader and may put them off contacting you.

When starting any piece, allow yourself to write and do not get caught up in editing your words as you go. This will help keep the tone conversational and you can review and amend it after you have completed the first draft.

Read your piece out loud. This may sound a little mad, but it is a great way to find out if your masterpiece flows, or if it needs some adjustment. It is amazing how different something sounds when you read it aloud rather than just in your head. Does it sound like you? Are you using your language and phrases? The idea is to let your personality shine through and let people get to know you. Your copy is all about building relationships as well as showcasing your knowledge and approach.

Proofread. Have a break from your copy before proofreading it. This way you are more likely to pick up any spelling or grammar mistakes. Do not rely on the spell and grammar check on your computer, it really is not good enough.

Certain marketing materials require extra care such as your website copy or a printed leaflet, so ask a friend to proofread it and give you feedback. Blog posts are a little more forgiving and if the content is good people will overlook an occasional misspelt word or incorrect grammar.

Repurpose your marketing

We are all aware of the environmental issues around rubbish on our planet and the importance of working to reduce waste and recycle where possible. Upcycling or repurposing items to give them a new lease of life is a great way to save precious resources. These ideas are transferable to your marketing, reuse and rework content to make the most of your hard work.

If you have been creating any form of marketing, you will know just how much time and effort goes into it. If everything you do is only used once, you are not making the most of your precious time or marketing assets.

Providing the same information in different formats is a great way to reach other groups of potential clients. Everyone has their preference on how they consume content, some like to read, others like watching videos or listening to podcasts. Presenting your information in a variety of ways means you are more likely to reach a wider audience.

Repurposing existing marketing takes less time than starting from scratch with new. It is a great way of working smarter and not harder! There are so many ways to repurpose marketing but you also want to make it as efficient as possible, there is a limit to what one person can do and be consistent with.

As a practitioner, I write a regular newsletter for my clients. I then upload the article from the newsletter onto the practice blog. This covers the article I need to create every month with minimal extra work. If the topic is relevant for my own website I will adapt it to be used there too.

Opportunities for repurposing blog content includes:

- Feature artwork and quotes to use on social media
- Use content in weekly emails
- Create a leaflet to give out at events or talks
- Build a presentation for talks or to share on other platforms
- Use the presentation slides to create a video
- Read or discuss the article and record it as a podcast or video
- Design an infographic to summarise the key points
- Create eBooks, guides, workshops, or books by collating articles

In Chapter 3, Reality check, you listed your existing marketing. Review what you already have and identify what worked best for you in terms of engagement or attracting clients. Use the analytics from your website or social media platforms to look for the most popular items. Pick your two or three best performing items and repurpose them into something else.

Whilst we all want to do everything, you will be setting yourself up to fail if you try and do it all at once. Decide what additional element you can create from your original content to give you another piece of marketing material. Once you get into the habit of creating the second piece of content, add to it with something else.

Finding inspiration

When you have a website you need to keep it fresh by consistently adding new content. You also need a flow of different ideas for your social media posts to keep people engaged. You know you should be blogging, making videos, creating images, or creating your newsletter, but it can be challenging even getting started. You find yourself sitting at your computer, staring at a blank screen or getting side-tracked by social media and before you know it you have been there for an hour and have achieved nothing!

Having a list of ideas and inspiration will stop you from getting stuck before you even get started. Once you know your topic it is much easier to create content. Here are a few places to find ideas for your marketing:

Client questions. Make a note of the questions you get asked on a regular basis and answer them in your marketing. Questions are a great way of generating relevant content for your audience. If you are being asked about something, Google is being asked too, so answering these will also help your SEO.

Share your stories. Tell your personal stories and allow people little insights into your world. You do not have to share everything, and some things are meant to stay private. People want to get to know you and telling stories is an incredibly powerful way to do this.

Books. I love reading and will often turn the corner of a page when I come across a brilliant insight or something that I can use to generate content for my audience. I will often start a post by sharing the name and author of a book that has inspired me. You could also do a book review if you have recently read something you think would be of interest to your favourite clients.

If a post you write was totally inspired by a particular book (or other work), make sure you reference it. This does not take away from your piece but instead shows that you are well-read, and it is good practice to give credit where credit is due.

Social media. Look for a quote or infographic that inspires you to write about the topic. Use it as inspiration and create your piece from your own perspective on the idea, adding in your own experience and knowledge.

Emails. Keep a reference folder of interesting emails and newsletters you receive. They will be from different people and across different types of business, but the common thing is they all contain a snippet of information that has sparked your interest. Use these to kick start an idea and see how it develops as you personalise it to you and your audience.

Update old content. You could freshen up an old article from your archives and bring it back to life. If you wrote something a few years ago your approach will have evolved, and you may have a completely different view on the topic now.

Reviews and comparisons. People love a review. How often do you look at the reviews on something before you decide to buy? You can review your favourite products and services and provide comparisons to other available options. People like honesty and will appreciate an informed opinion. An example of this could be the difference between buying herbs at the local health food store and getting them from a medical herbalist. Or the difference of going to a group yoga class and doing a one-to-one session with a yoga instructor experienced in working with a particular condition.

Social media groups. These are great places to find ideas or ask for inspiration. Look at the different topics being discussed, find one you have an opinion on and would be interesting to your clients.

Client stories and case studies. People buy people and there is nothing more powerful than the personal stories of your clients. These demonstrate their journey and how life has changed for them since working with you.

News stories. What is happening in the news that you can feature from your perspective and the service you offer?

EXERCISE: Content inspiration

Grab your notebook and spend ten minutes brainstorming different ideas you could use for creating interesting content for your clients. Do not allow yourself to overthink them, just write down anything that comes to mind.

Now review your list and circle the top ten ideas. These are the topics you can start to create your content around over the next few weeks and months which can be added to your editorial calendar, which we cover in the next section.

Editorial calendar

An editorial calendar is simply an outline of the marketing activities and topics you are planning to create over a period of time. Consistency is key with any marketing and by creating your calendar you will know exactly what content you want to produce, and when. This is especially important for online marketing where you should be producing regular content.

It will help bring your marketing recipe and the ingredients you need to life. Your yearly overview from Chapter 13, Marketing recipe, gives you an idea of what you want to achieve in your business each month, and you can then work out the different marketing recipes you need to do to support it. For example, if you are launching a workshop on joint pain you can start creating marketing to support the workshop in the run-up to it. You may want to write blog posts about related topics, create social media posts, share client stories or your own experience, and provide information on what your event will be like and why people should attend—the options are endless. The more you can tie your marketing into what you want to achieve in your business, the better it will perform for you.

If you do not have a specific event coming up and you are providing useful information you can use your inspiration list from the previous exercise. You can also use special dates, events, and holidays which are relevant to your business to produce content around.

Work a month at a time and create an overview of what you need to produce in your marketing using your yearly overview as a guide. You then take it a week at a time to plot out the ingredients required to make your recipes come to life and achieve your goals for your practice.

Remember the points below when you set your editorial calendar:

Focus on two or three strategies. Limit the number of different marketing strategies you do at a time, especially when you are starting out. Pick your main ones to focus on and get comfortable and consistent with those before trying to add any more to the mix.

Frequency. Work out how often you can realistically produce each type of content based on your schedule. It is better to be realistic about what you can achieve, even it is not as often as you would ideally like. The key is being consistent so if you are only able to write an article every two weeks, commit to that. It is better to do that than write a weekly article for one month and none the next.

What is your marketing goal? Making sure your content is tied to your goals and plan for your business. If you do not start with your goal in mind you will end up floundering, doing a bit of this and a bit of that, hoping something works.

Now it is time to get organised and create your content calendar. Double-check all your content fits the following criteria to make sure it is relevant:

- Does my content provide value to my clients?
- Am I providing clients with the next step to take?
- Is my content bringing value to my business and helping me achieve my goals?

Promote, promote, promote! Once you have created your content masterpiece, you need to promote it to make it reach as far as possible. Use your editorial calendar to work out what you will share and where you will share it week by week. Tell people about it by promoting it on social media and through your email list, basically use every outlet possible to let people know it exists.

Simple editorial calendar

Create your calendar in the best way that works for you and where you can easily access it. I use a planner, but a diary or spreadsheet will work just as well. Doing this will eliminate procrastination when it comes to creating your content as topics are decided in advance and deadlines are in place.

Start with an overview (see Table 4) of the month by picking your topics and make a note of any special dates or events you want to incorporate into your marketing:

Table 4: Editorial calendar—monthly overview

Month	September	Notes
Week 1	Healthy lunches for fussy children	Back to school
Week 2	Easy fast breakfasts on the go	
Week 3	Foods to celebrate the autumn equinox	Equinox
Week 4	Homemade edible present ideas— promote gift range	World School milk day Christmas gift launch
Week 5	Mini hampers of joy—promote gift range	

Then take a week at a time and plan out what you need to do each day (see Table 5):

Table 5: Editorial calendar—weekly plan

Day/date	Activity	Notes
Sunday		
Monday	Blog on healthy packed lunches—share on social media	
Tuesday	Email list with link to blog	Back to school
Wednesday	Social media—inspirational healthy lunch photo	
Thursday	Social media—poll on whether parents are happy with children's diet	
Friday	Social media—statistic about quality of lunches from blog	
Saturday	Networking with parents	Amber's party

You now know what you are doing every day and what needs to be created for the week ahead. You can get really organised and do it in advance or do your marketing day by day. If you are planning a holiday or have a particularly busy time coming up, an editorial calendar will take the pressure off and help you to stay consistent with your marketing.

EXERCISE: Your editorial calendar

Grab your notebook and using your yearly overview plan, marketing recipe and list of marketing inspirations, decide the main pieces of content you are going to create for your favourite clients for the next month. Then take the first week and work out what you will do each day. You can do more than a month at a time but it is best to start simple and find your flow. Download a template for your editorial calendar at helenharding.co.uk/bonus.

Understanding what works

Your marketing will take time to mature and for you to learn whether certain activities are viable. Discovering what actually works is the key to effective marketing. You can then stop doing the things that do not work and put all your time and resources into the things that do. The points below will help you discover what works and what does not:

What is the point of the activity? Who is your marketing for and what is it communicating? Having a goal and knowing what you are trying to achieve with your activities will help you focus your efforts on the right things. If you are just blasting information out there, you will be busy but get very little return on your time.

How did you hear about me? This is the question you should be asking everyone who enquires and every new client you work with. Track the answers you get so you start to build up a picture of where clients find out about you. This information is priceless and will help you decide where to focus your marketing efforts.

Understand your numbers. The number of different analytics available from online platforms can be pretty overwhelming. Tracking everything will become a chore, so keep it simple to help identify which marketing activities are working.

- **Email list.** Is your list growing? Seeing new people join your list each month is a good indication you are doing something right.
  - Emails opened—if you are using an email provider they will give you an overview of how well your emails are doing. Identify which ones have the best open rate. This shows which people on your list are actually interested in what you have to say. You will be able to see which topics and subject lines are popular and create more content around these subjects.
  - Emails clicked on—someone taking the time to click on a link in your email is the best indication of interest.
- **Social media.** Whilst the measures will vary on different platforms, you will find there are similarities. Do not look at your number of followers in isolation as it is a vanity measure. You could have thousands of followers but none of them are your ideal clients. Track this number in relation to the other measures.
  - Reach—how many people see your posts even if they do not interact with them?
  - Likes—do people like what you are sharing enough to leave a quick like?
  - Clicks—how many people click on your post to go on to do something else?
  - Shares—are people liking what you do enough to share it with their own connections?
  - Comments—which posts do people engage with enough to comment on?
- **Website traffic.** Have your website developer install Google Analytics on your website as it will allow you to see where people discover your website and what they do once they are there. Google Analytics will help you gauge how good your website is, if the quality is poor, people will not stick around.
  - New users—More new visitors show your website is attracting new people and reaching a wider audience.
  - Bounce rate—This is how many people come to your website and leave before they look at another page. This is the one number you want as low as possible, so be happy to see it go down.
  - Pages per session—The more pages they look at, the better.
  - Time on site—The longer people stay the more engaged they are with your content.

Track your numbers. Taking the time to note down your numbers each month will help you see where your efforts are paying off and highlight any areas you are neglecting. Knowing what is growing and where will help you decide if the activities are worth the effort you are putting in.

Briefing a designer

As a practitioner, you were probably not taught how to brief a designer or other creatives during your training. However, it is a hurdle you are likely to come up against in your business, especially when it comes to creating your marketing.

I was impressed by a therapist who had taken the initiative to out-source their logo and website design rather than try to put something together themselves. It was great that they recognised their limits and found a professional to do the job. However, it became challenging because the designer was not given a properly detailed brief, they were given free-range on the project with no direction other than the business name, discipline, and request to design a logo and website. Although they were paying a designer to come up with a beautiful design, the lack of a brief cost them dearly. The designer came up with what they thought was appropriate, but the designs were not right and led to several revisions which cost a lot of time and money.

Learning how to brief a creative will save you time and money as the job is far more likely to be right from the start and require few corrections. Making changes to a job can end up costing more than the original job so the more accurate the brief the cheaper the bill and the faster the turnaround.

Eight steps to writing a brief

1. Gather together your current marketing materials if you have any. Does it all work together or is it a miss-match of styles and colours?
2. Do your research and find examples of what you like in terms of colours, layouts, designs, style of pictures and fonts. Make a note of the things you hate too as this will give the creatives something to steer clear of.

3. Collate your examples and work out what you like best about them making notes and include links to any references.

4. Create a short overview of your business in terms of what you do and whom you work with so that the designer knows whom the finished designs need to appeal to. Include a copy of your brand guidelines if you have them. This is especially important if you are working with a new designer as they will need to understand your business.

5. Work out what items you need designed, for example, a logo, business cards, and website. Start with the minimum items you need as you can always build on them later.

6. Consider each item one at a time and work out what needs to be included on it. List everything required such as your logo, colours, fonts, pictures, and copy. I find creating a rough sketch helps me to work out how I want things to look and what I need to include in the brief.

7. You should get quotes from two or three designers, especially if the job is big and complicated. If you do not know any designers, ask for recommendations from your network and look at examples of their work to ensure you like their style before you commit. Agree on the price before you start any projects and make sure you know if corrections are included or whether they are charged as extra. If corrections are included, how many are allowed?

8. If you are providing copy, write it and get it double checked before supplying it to your designer. The more work you do upfront to minimise the likelihood of corrections the quicker and cheaper the job will be in the long run. Accuracy is especially important if you are printing something, as once it is done your only option is to reprint it if there are mistakes! As the saying goes, "check twice, print once"!

TAKEAWAY

You can learn to do many of the marketing activities yourself with time and practise. Maximise the return on your efforts with planning and repurposing what you create.

CASE STUDY

Name: Helen Diaz
Discipline: Mindset Coach and Therapist
Website: helendiaz.co.uk

Helen works as a full-time practitioner from four locations in the UK. She works with busy, stressed-out people who want more confidence, peace and happiness with sessions tailored to the individual getting them thinking, feeling and behaving differently.

Why did you decide to become a practitioner?

I wanted to help others! I had been working in the corporate world for 27 years where I was very lucky to be able to train in coaching and Neuro Linguistic Programming (NLP) and attend some incredible training programmes, for example a Tony Robbins weekend where I walked on fire which was an amazing experience. These experiences, along with being able to work with some very inspiring people allowed me to experience how much you can change your life and the life of others by sharing these amazing techniques.

As soon as the opportunity came up to do this, I grabbed it with both hands and took a year out to deepen my knowledge, get qualified and set up my business. I knew exactly what I wanted to do as a mindset coach and therapist.

What is your vision for your business?

I want to continue to grow my client base by experimenting and being creative with new offerings, while having more choice about the work I take on. I want to do less and be better at attracting the right clients who are on the same page as me.

I want to continue adding in aspects that build other skills and be open to other opportunities such as becoming a tutor and examiner for a practitioner college I studied at.

What are the three most important things to date that have helped you grow your business?

1. I just got started and accepted everything does not have to be perfect. I created a simple website and started working with clients for free whilst I was training to build my confidence and experience.

2. I made sure I spent time working on my business as well as in it, it is important to get the balance right. It is easy to think if I build it, they will come, but they will not.

3. I thought of marketing as an experiment and signed up for all the free marketing, talks and courses to learn, but I only did what spoke to me and fitted.

4. I got listed on directories and regularly reviewed my profiles, making a note of any changes I made. This helped me to see what works and to make sure the listings were paying for themselves with the enquiries I received.

5. I put my prices up every year in January, you have to own your value!

With hindsight, is there anything you would have done differently?

I wish I had done more experimentation and worried less and stopped constantly questioning myself. I now know to give things a go and see what happens.

Perhaps I would have experimented more with leaflets, advertisements and networking and realised that as long as I got a booking that paid for it, it was a successful piece of marketing. I really worried that my marketing may not hit the mark, but I once I received the advice about it is just an experiment and kept tweaking and trialling, I felt much happier to put myself out there.

What's next for your business?

I will continue to be creative about what I offer my clients and to learn more techniques to enhance my skills such as a workshop for post-traumatic stress disorder (PTSD) which both interests me and fits with the work and clients I enjoy working with.

CHAPTER EIGHTEEN

Making it Happen

B oring as it may sound, creating good habits and putting the right processes in places will support you in creating a sustainable, thriving practice. Incorporating these into your life, marketing, and business are the best ways to make sure things happen, consistently. You do not need big fancy systems and lots of technology, keep things as simple as possible to make the most of your precious time.

Focus

There is incredible power to be gained by learning to focus with your marketing. As a practitioner, you probably require clients to focus on themselves outside of their appointments with exercises, supplements, diets, journaling, or meditation to achieve the results they want. Why would your marketing be any different?

Focus on one big goal or project at a time, you cannot expect to build a website, design a workshop, and write a book at the same time. You will of course have your day to day business and marketing activities to keep on top of but concentrate on your big projects one at a time or you will spread yourself too thin.

This is a lesson I learnt the hard way having spent years starting lots of different projects, all important in their own right and beneficial to my business. Unfortunately jumping from one thing to another got me nowhere fast! I read two books which finally woke me up, *Essentialism* by Greg McKeown (2014) and *The One Thing* by Gary Keller with Jay Papasan (2012). The reality of jumping around from one thing to another not only means you do not finish anything, but you are really inefficient with your time. The person who starts ten different tasks will only make a tiny progression on each. Whereas the person who starts one and focuses on it until it is finished will always be more productive and actually complete projects. Below are ways to improve your focus:

Pick your priority. Decide which project you are going to focus on, you cannot do them all.

Be realistic. If you have a tendency to overestimate what you are able to achieve in a day, start by selecting your number one priority and focus on that. If you get onto other jobs from your list, bonus!

Let go! Do not allow yourself to think you can do everything, you are only human after all! Make peace with letting things go and accept that things cannot always be done perfectly, good enough has to suffice sometimes. Another thing to let go of is the need to try and control everything. The calmer you can be around things that are outside of your control, the better.

Cut out the distractions. Tell your colleagues or family not to disturb you. Turn off your email and put your phone in aeroplane mode, limit anything that could draw you away from the task in hand.

Celebrate what you achieve. The more you celebrate the small wins, the more they will grow and become the big wins. Doing this each day will help you appreciate what you have achieved and recognise the progress you are making.

RECOMMENDED READING: *Essentialism* **by Greg McKeown**

This book is all about simplifying your life so that you regain control of everything and put your energy into the things that really matter.

RECOMMENDED READING: *The One Thing*
by Gary Keller with Jay Papasan

A brilliant book on productivity and the art of focusing on one thing at a time and achieving more in less time whilst staying on track with your projects.

Simplify things

This does not have to be limited to your business. Simplifying areas of your personal life will release time for you to use elsewhere. Start by taking a long look at what currently takes up your time and energy in any given day or week. Why do you do what you do?

You may find you do some things out of habit and the reality is they are not urgent or in some cases even needed. You have just accepted they are part of your routine to the point where you stop questioning them. They can be cut from your routine straight away and this will give you an immediate return of available time. If there is a true purpose behind something you do work out if there is a way you can make it easier.

Ask yourself:

- Does it make sense?
- Does it need to be this hard?
- Where am I making things complicated?
- How can I make things quicker?

Avoid making impulsive decisions as it can end up making things more complicated. If you rush into a decision, you can easily make the wrong decision. I completely fell into this trap with a piece of software that promised to revolutionise my business. I watched a webinar and to get the bonus gifts signed up there and then. It is a well-known sales technique that works on our fear of missing out and even though I knew that was exactly what was happening, it got me! Fast forward two years and I ended up cancelling my subscription as I struggled to make the software work for me and never even used the bonuses! What a waste of money and it niggled at me because I was aware that I was not utilising the software but it was still costing my business money.

Sometimes simple just means pause for a while and sit with it. Decide based on what you need now, rather than the promise of great things to come.

Start with simple

When you start projects, do them with the aim of keeping things simple, you will then be able to manage them much more easily as they develop. Work out the minimum that you need to do, do that and do it well. We complicate things by constantly doing more, adding more, and overthinking everything. Keeping things simple is about removing what is not required in order to get to the things that are important.

Declutter your to-do list

How long is your to-do list right now? Are you adding more than you are crossing off? Is it formed of several different lists?

If you have a list full of stuff that you have to, need to, must, or should do, you are using it as a way of beating yourself up. It will keep you stuck in a busy cycle and feeling overwhelmed. It is time to detox your to-do list and create a manageable one where you feel like you are actually achieving something. Take ten minutes with your to-do list and ask yourself the following questions:

Does this have to be done? Often, our to-do lists are often full of things that we would like to do or it would be nice to do but are not necessary. They are more of a wish list or even things you have been thinking about doing but have not decided yet. Really, these are ideas and while you want to make a note of them they should not be on your to-do list. Create a separate list to store your ideas safely for future reference.

If it is a yes, does it need to be done now, or can it be done later? Not everything on the list will be equal. There will be things on your list which are not your priority and not where you should be putting your focus. Identify those jobs that are not needed this week so you can separate out what you need to do now.

Can I change the deadlines? If you are under pressure because of a looming deadline is it something you can defer? Whilst you do not want to be late on something, it may be possible to move a deadline to take the pressure off. You will do a much better job if you feel calm and not stressed out. Whilst you do not want to let anyone down, especially if you are working on a project that involves others, it is far better to do this ahead of time and give people warning so you are not letting them down at the last minute.

Do I need to do this? As small business owners, we wear a lot of different hats and can be martyrs when it comes to our business. You get bogged down feeling like you must do everything. Before you know it, things start falling through the cracks.

Work out which jobs you could hand to someone else to do. This can be as simple as getting help with household chores or finding support with your admin. Anything you can delegate in your personal or work life will give you time.

Get a good routine

If you feel like you are constantly jumping from one task to another and getting frustrated at how little you are achieving, take a look at your routine. Do you have set times for work? Do you include time for working on your business as well as in it?

If you do not, schedule time in your diary for these activities and start to build good routines and habits. You will find not only do you get a lot more done as you have focused time, but you also will not feel as overwhelmed.

Make sure you book some breaks into your routines too as you will not be able to focus for hours at a time. So, get yourself into a good routine and start reaping the rewards of achieving more, being less stressed, and having the freedom to do the things you love outside of your business.

Creating checklists

We all have jobs which we need to repeat over and over again in our business. These are the tasks you have become so familiar with; you can do them without thinking. Then there are the ones which have to be worked out each time you start.

Checklists or procedures are simply a list of stages you go through in order to get a job done including any references to make the job easier. Whilst they can take time to compile, they are an asset to your business and will be well worth the effort in the future. You probably already have a selection of different lists you use as a reference within your profession such as scripts or case history forms to help you do a great job. Creating these checklists is simply adding to them to help your business to run smoothly.

Creating checklists for all your repeatable tasks stops you from having to try and remember exactly what to do each time you start a job. It will provide you with the steps and any references or information needed to help you complete them efficiently. It will make sure you do not miss out any key steps and reduces the number of mistakes made in the process. A huge advantage is when you get to a position where you want to delegate or outsource a task, you will have a reference file you can provide making the transition much easier.

EXERCISE: Your checklists

Grab your notebook and write down the jobs you do regularly which would benefit from having a checklist. The next time you do one, take the time to write down the stages as you go. See this as an ongoing project and make sure you maintain your checklists as your business evolves and develops.

Batching

Batching is a way of being super productive and is simply doing similar tasks together. It will save you a serious amount of time and stress. Anything that frees up time is worth doing in my book, and batching is one of the best ways I have found to do this.

When you stop and start different tasks there is a time delay between them. Whether it is getting your brain in gear or logging into different websites, there is a time cost. If you reduce the number of times you move between one thing and another, it will significantly add up during the day.

It is easier to get into the flow of jobs when you are focusing on them. You will not have to work out where you got to or try to remember what to do next because you are in the right zone for the task in hand. Batching will help you to clear the tasks that can often take days or weeks to get around to. It is a great way to give you space to work on your projects or take downtime with family and friends without having the unfinished to-do list hanging over you.

Do not limit batching to work. Batching some of your home activities and chores you can save even more time. It is a way of working efficiently in every area to free you up for the things you love to do.

Here are some ideas to start you thinking about what you can batch:

- **Clients**. Book your client appointments or calls together so you can get fully into the practitioner zone. A good way of doing this is to only work with clients on set days each week, leaving the others for projects, marketing or having fun.
- **Marketing**. Whether you produce blogs, podcasts, videos, or social media, the more you can do these activities together, the better. Especially if you have equipment to set up or want to do your hair and makeup before appearing on video, or you need to clear an area to work, batching will be a huge time saver.
- **Social media**. Create your posts for the week (or month) in one go and use a scheduling tool to automate their delivery. You will still need to check them and respond to any comments, but you can check-in and do this a couple of times a day.
- **Emails**. Only check your emails at set times a day, do not dip in and out of them as soon as you see the little notification. If you do not trust yourself not to look, turn off your notifications or close the programme down.
- **Administration**. Do all your accounts and other similar administrative tasks together. This way they will not interfere in your day to day work.
- **Planning**. Whether you are planning a trip of a lifetime or the next year of your practice, if you want to progress quickly it is much easier to work on them in allocated chunks of time.
- **Chores**. Rather than doing jobs as you go, batch similar chores together so you do them in one hit.
- **Errands**. How can you batch together trips, so you only go out once? I have learnt to be a lot better at this since moving to a rural area. It is 5 miles to our local town, so I make the most of trips by shopping, getting my hair cut, filling the car up, or meeting friends in one trip.
- **Dinners**. If you are cooking a meal, make extra portions and freeze them so you have your own tasty ready meals. Create a meal plan at

the start of the week so you are not thinking about what you eat each day. It will save you decision time and you will have a shopping list ready.

- **Friends and family.** Making a couple of visits in one afternoon or making a few phone calls in an evening is a great way to catch up with people and be efficient with your time.

Batching requires some organisation but will be well worth the effort. These are the steps:

1. Work out which tasks you are going to batch and roughly how much time you will need for each.
2. Create blocks of time and put them on your calendar so you have time specifically allocated for each batch of tasks.
3. Remove all other distractions when you are working on these tasks. Make sure you use your time productively and do not get side-tracked.

TAKEAWAY

Pick your most important big project and focus on it until it is finished.

CHAPTER NINETEEN

When the Going Gets Tough

Building a business is challenging, it will bring up every one of your personal demons and you will often feel like you take one step forward and two back. It is the best personal development activity ever and will magnify all your fears and insecurities. It will test you to the limit, you will be crying in despair and wanting to throw it all in one day and flying as high as a kite the next.

You may be the best practitioner and have the best business strategies but it is just as important to work on your mindset. If you do not have the right mindset to deal with the challenges that running your own business will throw up then you may become stuck and sabotage your success. You think you have dealt with something and as you take the next step, the old demons come right back to test your reserve and try to tempt you back into hiding.

See these challenges as just part of the journey and recognise that your brain will react against anything that does not feel safe and comfortable. Anything it perceives as scary will set off the alarm bells and it will automatically try and keep you in your comfort zone. When everything in the Universe moves towards change, why do we get so uncomfortable around our own growth? Getting stuck in your comfort zone is a place you can hide but it will never be a place you will flourish in.

179

Unfortunately, this was a lesson I learnt rather late in life. My inner "Captain Sensible" likes to feel safe and secure so I spent far too long stuck in my various comfort zones. I worked for the same company for over 20 years, stayed in relationships way too long, and I lived in my first house for 13 years to mention a few.

When life threw me several challenges in a short period of time I was forced unceremoniously from my comfort zone. I soon found out things were not as bad as I had feared. It was the stories I had constantly told myself that kept me stuck. Although uncomfortable at first, once I addressed my mindset and started moving forward again things got easier. I am still a work in progress; I am only human! Knowing some of the big ways I sabotage myself and having ways to work through it is the difference between floundering and thriving.

Staying the same is not an option when change is one thing in life that is guaranteed. Although this book is about building a sustainable business in your way and playing to your strengths, you will still have to step outside of your comfort zone to thrive. This is where the mindset work comes in and will help you to move through the challenges and flourish.

Success saboteurs

There are all sorts of ways we sabotage ourselves when we are doing the important, scary work. By understanding your own sabotaging habits, patterns, and behaviours, you can do something about them rather than just letting them continue, get in the way and stop you thriving. Awareness is the first step to changing any unhelpful habits and patterns. Being aware of the different ways you can sabotage your success will help you to navigate them as they happen. We have looked at a few of the saboteurs along the way and here are a few of the big ones that may get in your way and stop you from reaching your potential.

Perfectionism

This is at the top of the list of saboteurs and it is something that kept me stuck and playing small for far too many years. Recognising how perfection affected every aspect of my life lead me to train as a practitioner, and learning how to address it was one of the most empowering things I did. My inner perfectionist does come out to play occasionally but I now have ways to put her back in her box, so she is no longer able to create the chaos she once did.

Many of my clients try to argue that perfection is good and all about quality and excellence. Brené Brown in *Daring Greatly* brilliantly describes what perfection is not:

> Perfectionism is not the same thing as striving for excellence. Perfectionism is not about healthy achievement and growth. It's the belief that if we do things perfectly and look perfect, we can minimise or avoid the pain of blame, judgement, and shame. Perfectionism is a twenty-tonne shield that we lug around, thinking it will protect us, when in fact it's the thing that's really preventing us from being seen.

> (Brown, 2015, p. 128)

Brené goes on to say:

> Perfectionism is not the key to success. In fact, research shows that perfectionism hampers achievement. Perfectionism is correlated with depression, anxiety, addiction, and life paralysis or missed opportunities. The fear of failing, making mistakes, not meeting people's expectations, and being criticized keeps us outside of the arena where healthy competition and striving unfolds.

> (Brown, 2015, p. 129)

Perfection can play out in many ways and for some people they only become perfectionists when they are stressed. For others it is almost an addictive compulsion. There is a lot of fear around being judged so when it comes to your business and your marketing, as a perfectionist, you can spend your time constantly re-visiting something, tweaking, and trying to make it absolutely perfect. This results in perfectionists often having many unfinished projects, instead they avoid any criticism and stay safe and hidden in their comfort zone.

The Pareto principle or 80/20 rule brilliantly demonstrates just how inefficient being a perfectionist can be. The principle maintains that 20 per cent of effort will achieve 80 per cent of the desired outcome. To put the 80 per cent into context, it would be a first if you were at university doing a bachelor's degree, so it is by no means a poor standard. A perfectionist will then waste the next 80 per cent of their time trying to perfect it (see Figure 3).

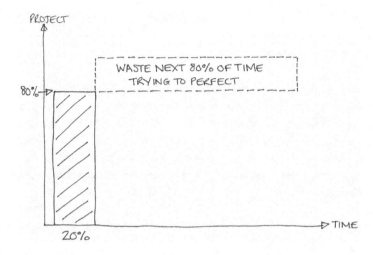

Figure 3: Time wasted through perfectionism.

We know there is no such thing as perfect, so trying to do something perfectly is trying to do the impossible. Instead, stop once you achieve 80 per cent and ask yourself the question, "does it do the job?" If you answer yes at this point, move onto the next thing. You will achieve five times the output if you recognise when a piece of work is good enough compared to carrying on refining and tweaking the original piece. This could be the difference in writing a months' worth of articles in the same time as it takes to write one article (nearly) perfectly (see Figure 4)!

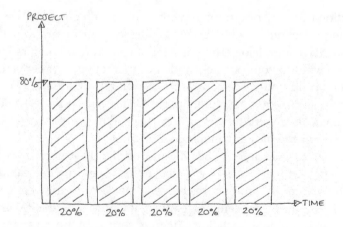

Figure 4: Productivity potential by stopping perfection.

If you have a lot of fear around letting something go, check what stories you are telling yourself. There may be some internal work you need to do around this, either using your preferred mindset techniques or getting assistance from your practitioner or coach.

RECOMMENDED READING: *The Gifts of Imperfection* by Brené Brown

As a researcher in shame and vulnerability, and from her own experiences, Brené has uncovered an insight into perfection. This book looks at letting go of whom you think you are supposed to be and instead embrace who you are. Her remedy to perfection is to live a wholehearted life by adopting courage, compassion and connection.

Procrastination

This can be a major symptom of perfection when you are facing something that scares you or one of those boring chores I like to call "necessary evils" which we all have to do at times. When you procrastinate, you are avoiding acting on the things that are most important. This can manifest itself in many ways such as getting side-tracked by social media, doing the cleaning, or going out for a coffee; basically anything that distracts you from the important things you should be doing instead.

I discovered I can be a master procrastinator if left unchallenged. When I had a task that scared me and took me outside of my comfort zone, I got very busy. I could easily find ways of distracting myself and it is amazing how therapeutic decluttering a drawer can be instead of knuckling down and getting my head around the task in hand. The problem with these busy tasks is they disguise themselves as being relevant jobs. You can justify why you are doing them but really, they are just tricksters and they are keeping you from working on the priorities that will take your business forward. No matter how well you can justify the need to perform these jobs, they are not your priority and are, ultimately, a distraction.

So often, being busy is mistaken as a sign of success when really it is just a place that we hide in when we are procrastinating, feeling overwhelmed, or scared. If you find that you are constantly busy and you are not achieving what you need to, it is time to drop the busy badge and get focused on what will make a difference to you and your business.

Other procrastination tricks are constantly daydreaming, wondering, and planning how everything will be when your business is flourishing. You have loads of ideas, but nothing gets acted on and before you know it another month or year has passed, you are in exactly the same position and everything is still a dream.

EXERCISE: Procrastination awareness

Grab your notebook and answer the following questions:

- What is your go-to procrastination habit when you should be working on your business?
- What are the things you do to avoid the important or scary jobs?

This awareness will help you to quickly recognise when you are avoiding the important work. You can then make the choice to re-focus your efforts on the right things.

RECOMMENDED READING: *Finish* **by Jon Acuff**

This is a brilliantly practical book which will help you combat perfection and procrastination and actually finish the projects you start.

Shiny marketing syndrome

This is another saboteur that keeps us busy but achieving little from our hard work other than being constantly busy with marketing activities. When it comes to marketing, there are generally two camps:

1. Those who jump from one thing to another, constantly changing strategies
2. Those who focus on two or three key strategies until they get results

Which camp are you in? If you do not have any clients, it is most likely to be the first one and you are being seduced by shiny marketing syndrome. This is where you find yourself bouncing around, trying all the new and different tactics, hoping something will eventually work. If you find you are easily lured into trying out the next new "thing" or getting side-tracked by a new social media platform, you are not alone. I have bought my share of courses that will provide "the answer" and ended up not finishing them, or even worse not even starting them.

Jumping around like this will get you nowhere fast. It is eating up your time, energy, and money and you will be left still struggling for clients. Before long frustration sneaks in and you start to resent doing any marketing. Even worse, you could fall out of love with your business, believing it is not possible to thrive. I have seen amazing practitioners want to give up because they have tried really, really hard, and still did not manage to find any clients. The problem was they were jumping around desperately from one thing to another and not doing anything consistently or well.

This is why it is so important to keep it simple, decide what you are going to do, create your recipe, and start cooking up consistent marketing. This is the only way you will start to see results from your marketing and know what is working for you.

Putting the needs of others first

This is particularly challenging for practitioners who are naturally caring people and want to help others. It is very easy to find yourself constantly running around looking after others to the detriment of your own life and priorities. How many times have you found yourself saying "yes" to things when every cell in your body was shouting "no"? Times when you committed yourself to something and regretted the decision afterwards because you just knew it was not right for you. Ultimately you feel frustrated with yourself and with others for taking advantage of you. If you are not careful, you can end up using all your time and energy on other people's requests.

There is a story I tell my clinical clients based on the chapter "If Someone Throws You the Ball, You Don't Have to Catch It" from *Don't Sweat the Small Stuff* by Richard Carlson.

My shortened version goes something like this: Many of our inner struggles come from our tendency to jump on board someone else's problem. Someone throws you a concern (the metaphoric ball) and you assume you must catch it and try and solve it for them. Later you feel stressed when you are behind and resentful that everyone is making demands on you. You forget about your willing participation in the situation.

Instead of automatically catching the ball, you can choose whether you want to or not. It is not your ball and you do not have to catch it, but there will be times when you want to catch it. The same idea applies to someone throwing a comment at you or criticising you, it is their ball, but you decide to catch it, or let it go. So, next time someone throws something to you, take a moment and decide if you want to catch it, or simply say to yourself "not my ball" and let it go. (Carlson, 1998, p. 219)

EXERCISE: Personal boundaries

In your notebook, write a list of the people in your life whose needs constantly come before yours? Work out who needs to be a priority (although it does not mean they should always come first) such as dependents, and who are not. I am sure there will be a few people who may shout loud but who are not your priority. Who in this list can you say "no" to in the future?

Are there any balls you can drop? This could buy you back some precious time and energy too.

Scarcity mindset

A scarcity mindset is when you focus on what you do not have, rather than what you do. It shows up when you miss opportunities, feel defeated, and believe you cannot be successful. Scarcity creates a lot of anxiety and stress and can creep into all areas of your life, health, and work. It can cause jealousy when you start to compare yourself to others, assuming they are doing better or have more of what you want.

You start to protect what you have out of fear and focus on surviving or getting by. You may tell yourself there will never be enough time, money, clients, and the list goes on. The fear holds you back and this focus means you miss out on opportunities that present themselves because you are only attending to the immediate things.

If you are doing well and have a scarcity mindset you will feel it is never enough, and operating from a place of scarcity leaves you feeling fragile. Every new client has the potential to make or break your business and every decision to spend money matters. It is a surefire way to always feel like you are constantly struggling and never flourishing.

EXERCISE: Creating an abundant mindset

What are you saying to yourself about money or clients from a place of scarcity? Listen out for sentences that come from a place of fear such as "I can't afford…" and write them down in your notebook. Think about how you can change your language to make it useful, for example "this is not my priority right now".

Create affirmations around what you want to believe and achieve and repeat them to yourself regularly. Surround yourself with reminders of your affirmations on sticky notes or screen savers to keep reinforcing them to yourself.

Have a clear-out and let go of things you have been hanging onto just in case you may need them. This will create space for the new abundance to flow into your life and business.

RECOMMENDED READING: *Get Rich Lucky Bitch* by Denise Duffield-Thomas

This practical book will help you address the blocks you have around money so you can start to invite wealth and abundance into your life and business.

Stopping the sabotage

Most of the saboteurs are underpinned by different fears that surface and threaten to stop you in your tracks. Unfortunately, running a business will press lots of fear buttons and you will be on an emotional rollercoaster at times but the feeling you will get from your achievements will far outweigh the challenges you face. Sometimes you just have to dig deep and carry on.

There are lots of ways to deal with any challenges that arise. Use some of the suggestions below, or your own favourite techniques, to help you deal with the challenges. If you find deeper issues keep coming up, seek help from your chosen practitioner or coach to work through them, or you will be going around in circles.

Awareness. What are your default sabotaging behaviour(s) and habits? What do you find you do automatically when you have a challenge outside your comfort zone? Notice what stories you tell yourself around these and the beliefs that are hiding behind them. Awareness is the first step to changing things. Use the lists you have compiled in your notebook to help you build your awareness around your automatic sabotaging behaviours and stories.

Write your thoughts down. Get everything down on paper to stop them from whirling around your head. Looking at them in black and white will help you to gain some perspective over what you are thinking.

Reflect. What are the consequences of continuing this behaviour? A great question to ask yourself is, "is this useful?". Often it will not be as it is just your fear trying to keep you safe. Learn from this situation but do not spend ages analysing it. Instinctively you will know what is right for you so listen in to what your intuition is trying to tell you.

Talk it through. If necessary, reach out to your support network and talk through the situation and how you are feeling. Just saying the words out loud to someone will help you get clarity over what is going on and find the answers you need. Your business buddy or friend can also provide you with feedback and suggestions if appropriate.

Decide. Recognise that you have a choice and only one opportunity to use your time, it is your most precious commodity and you will never get it back. Make a conscious decision on what to spend your time on and write it down using positive, descriptive language. This will provide you with the direction to move towards. Now work out a plan of action for making this happen that fits in with you and your life.

Be kind to yourself. Appreciate and recognise what you have achieved so far and the work you put into it. Reflect on your confidence boosters from Chapter 2, Setting you up for success. Write up some affirmations and use them regularly to reinforce who you are, what you deserve and what you want to achieve. Make friends with yourself and get comfortable with your quirks. If you find yourself unfairly comparing yourself to others you need to assess if this is a realistic assessment or are you just being too hard on yourself? Remember you are your own harshest critic and chances are you are being too sensitive and what you see is not noticed by others.

Act. The antidote for fear is action. Take your plan of action and work out what your first step is and take it. It may feel a little uncomfortable at first, but this shows that you are stretching yourself and growing. For added accountability, share your plan with a trusted friend or business buddy so they can help to keep you on track if they see you are sabotaging yourself.

Get help. Rather than muddling through and getting stuck, get help and address any outstanding challenges and issues you have. Do whatever it takes to stop the sabotaging fears and habits and allow yourself to flourish.

Work on your mindset. Work to build your confidence and resilience in the areas where you struggle. Make reflection and gratitude part of your day, recognise what you have achieved and how far you have come.

Surround yourself with supportive people. Surround yourself with people that reinforce what you want to achieve. Make sure you keep the company of like-minded people who will support you and help you to become the thriving practitioner that you deserve to be.

Treat others as inspiration for you. Recognise areas where you become stuck in your life and business by comparing yourself to others. Look at the people you are comparing yourself with and think of them as examples of what you want to work towards, and what is possible.

TAKEAWAY

Working on your, mindset and anything that could sabotage you, is as critical to your success as being good at what you do, and knowing how to market yourself.

CHAPTER TWENTY

Over to You!

W e have come to the end of our journey through this book together. You have the foundations you need to build your thriving, sustainable practice, your way.

By now, I hope you recognise the best way to do this is to create your own recipe, one that works to your strengths and suits you, your life, and your business.

You have to be consistent and keep showing up. There will be times when it is easy and others where it feels like an uphill struggle, but you have the tools to sort them out and get back on track again.

Take things one step at a time, make sure you have the foundations in place for your business and start to build a practice that you are proud of and that reflects your values and you as a practitioner.

You can always go back on sections. Do not try and do everything at once. And remember to always question why you are doing something when it comes to your marketing.

Download your free templates and resources to help you with the exercises in this book: helenharding.co.uk/bonus

Marketing is all about building relationships and I would love to connect with you.

- Website: helenharding.co.uk
- Email: helen@helenharding.co.uk
- Social media: helenhardinguk

Bye for now!
Helen

CHAPTER TWENTY ONE

Resources

I have compiled a list of the resources mentioned throughout this book and a few more which have inspired and educated my clients and me.

I have summarised some of my favourite books to help you decide which ones to read whilst working on specific areas of your marketing. I have also guided you to internet resources to help you set up and run your business.

Books—marketing

Building a Story Brand: Clarify Your Message So Customers Will Listen by Donald Miller

Learn the seven elements of great storytelling to change the way you talk about the work you do and connect with your clients. The book provides you with a framework to work through and change the way you communicate.

How the World Sees You: Discover Your Highest Value Through the Science of Fascination by Sally Hogshead

Learn how to succinctly communicate your qualities by discovering how others see you and the true value you provide them. The aim is to unlearn being boring where you have camouflaged yourself to blend in and instead learn how to stand out using the science and art of fascination.

Talk Triggers: The Complete Guide to Creating Customers with Word of Mouth by Jay Baer and Daniel Lemin

This book walks you through the steps of creating a word of mouth strategy for your business. It includes lots of case studies from different sized companies for inspiration and to demonstrate how effective the strategy, no matter the size of your business.

This is Marketing: You Can't be Seen Until You Learn to See by Seth Godin

This book shows marketing is not about making noise but about building trust and relationships. Truly powerful marketing is grounded in generosity and empathy and solves the problems of your clients.

Wellpreneur: The Ultimate Guide for Wellness Entrepreneurs to Nail Your Niche and Find Clients Online by Amanda Cook

If you want to create digital products as an additional income stream for your business and learn how to market yourself online, then this book is for you as it is written specifically for practitioners. Amanda walks you through her "Organic Growth System" to set up your health and well-being business online.

Your Press Release is Breaking My Heart: A Totally Unconventional Guide to Selling Your Story in the Media by Janet Murray

This book walks you through the process of getting press coverage for your business step-by-step. Specifically written to teach small businesses how to do their own PR and stand out in a sea of bland pitches to journalists and media owners to get their story noticed.

Books—mindset and productivity

Essentialism: The Disciplined Pursuit of Less by Greg McKeown

Learn how to identify the things that really matter in all areas of your life and focus on those. From the pursuit of less you regain control of your choices, reduce stress, and make life simple.

Finish: Give Yourself the Gift of Done by Jon Acuff

This is a brilliantly practical book to help you combat perfection so you can actually get your projects finished and out into the world.

Get Rich Lucky Bitch: Release Your Money Blocks and Live a First Class Life by Denise Duffield-Thomas

This practical book will help you address the blocks you have around money so you can start to invite wealth and abundance into your life and business.

The Gifts of Imperfection: Let Go of Who You Think You're Supposed to Be and Embrace Who You Are by Brené Brown

As a researcher in shame and vulnerability, and from her own experiences, Brené has uncovered an insight into perfection which resonated strongly with me. This book explores letting go of whom you think you are supposed to be and instead embrace who you are. Her remedy to perfection is to live a wholehearted life by adopting courage, compassion, and connection.

The One Thing: The Surprisingly Simple Truth Behind Extraordinary Results by Gary Keller with Jay Papasan

A brilliant book on productivity and the art of focusing on one thing at a time and achieving more in less time whilst staying on track with your projects.

Internet resources and links

Advertising Standards Authority (ASA)

Website: www.asa.org.uk (last accessed 28th August 2019)

This the United Kingdom's independent regulator of advertising across all media. They apply the advertising codes, which are written by the Committees of Advertising Practice (CAP). Their work includes acting on complaints and proactively checking the media to act against misleading, harmful or offensive advertising.

Companies House

Website: www.gov.uk/government/organisations/companies-house (last accessed 28th August 2019)

A subsection of the gov.uk website which administers the legal framework in which UK companies are run. If you are setting up a limited company, it allows you to check the availability of and secure your chosen business name.

British Chambers of Commerce (BCC)

Website: www.britishchambers.org.uk (last accessed 28th August 2019)

The BCC is the organisation at the centre of a nationwide network of Chambers of Commerce. Through their local branches they support member businesses of all sizes by lobbying, partnering with relevant organisations and organising events.

The Federation of Small Businesses (FSB)

Website: www.fsb.org.uk (last accessed 28th August 2019)

The FSB is an organisation whose mission is to help small businesses thrive. They offer members a wide range of services including access to free business banking and a library of business fact sheets and documents. They also offer access to events such as networking and masterclasses.

Google My Business (GMB)

Website: www.google.com/business (last accessed 28th August 2019)

GMB allows you to manage how you appear in Google searches and maps. The GMB pages allow Google to provide answers to its users in one place without having to go off and visit different websites, so you need to make sure you are listed. Follow the step-by-step instructions to set up and update your page.

Government services and information (United Kingdom)

Website: www.gov.uk (last accessed 28th August 2019)

All government departments, public bodies and agencies are housed on this website. You will find areas that are related to both your business and personal needs. Some of the sections are invaluable for working with clients. You will need to register to use certain services for example filing a tax return and you may have to register your business separately.

Information available includes the following areas:

- Benefits
- Business, self-employment, and company formation
- Childcare and parenting
- Disabled people
- Education and learning
- Employing people
- Environment and countryside
- Housing and local services
- Money and tax (HMRC)
- Medicines and healthcare product regulations
- Working, jobs, and pensions

Health and Safety Executive (HSE)

Website: www.hse.gov.uk (last accessed 28th August 2019)

The HSE provides the regulatory framework for health and safety within the workplace. You are responsible for health and safety in your business and the laws are there to protect you, your employees, and the public from workplace dangers.

Information Commissioners Office (ICO)

Website: www.ico.org.uk (last accessed 28th August 2019)

Set up to uphold information rights in the public interest also known as data protection. If you are handling personal information (as a practitioner you are), you are legally required to sign-up to and maintain strict data protection guidelines.

Local Authority (LA) website

Your LA website will provide you with contact details of departments you may have to consult before setting up your business. They are also a great resource for what is happening in your neighbourhood.

Medicines and Healthcare products Regulatory Agency (MHRA)

Website: www.gov.uk/government/organisations/medicines-and-healthcare-products-regulatory-agency (last accessed 28th August 2019)

Part of the gov.uk website, the MHRA section provides information on products related to healthcare and medicines, for example, information on the regulatory status of different herbs and devices. These pages are particularly useful for practitioners involved in the retailing of herbs.

Princes Trust

Website: www.princes-trust.org.uk (last accessed 28th August 2019)

This is a charity set up to help young people (18–30) to get their lives on track. Enterprise is the name of their scheme aimed at helping people to set up their own business. If you need to produce a full business plan to apply for funding or another reason, they have brilliant free templates and guides which will help you through the process.

BIBLIOGRAPHY AND REFERENCES

Acuff, J. (2017). *Finish: Give Yourself the Gift of Done*. New York, NY: Portfolio/Penguin.

All-Party Parliamentary Group for Integrated Healthcare (2018). *MPs want complementary, traditional and natural medicine to rescue NHS from financial crisis* [Press Release]. 13 December 2018. Available at: https://www.yourhealthyourchoice.com.au/news-features/mps-want-complementary-traditional-and-natural-medicine-to-rescue-health-system-from-financial-crisis/ (last accessed: 5 January 2020).

Baer, J. and Lemin, D. (2018). *Talk Triggers: The Complete Guide to Creating Customers with Word of Mouth*. New York, NY: Portfolio/Penguin.

Brown, B. (2010). *The Gifts of Imperfection: Let Go of Who You Think You're Supposed to Be and Embrace Who You Are*. Minnesota: Hazelden.

Brown, B. (2015). *Daring Greatly: How the Courage to Be Vulnerable Transforms the Way We Live, Love, Parent, and Lead*. London: Portfolio/Penguin.

Carlson, R. (1998). *Don't Sweat the Small Stuff and it's all Small Stuff: Simple Ways to Keep the Little Things from Taking Over Your Life*. London: Hodder and Staunton.

Cook, A. (2017). *Wellpreneur: The Ultimate Guide for Wellness Entrepreneurs to Nail Your Niche and Find Clients Online*. s.l.: Yacum Hill Press.

199

Ducker, C. (2017). *Rise of the Youpreneur: The Definitive Guide to Becoming the Go-To Leader in Your Industry and Building a Future—Proof Business.* Cambridge: 4C Press.

Duffield-Thomas, D. (2013). *Get Rich, Lucky Bitch! Release Your Money Blocks and Live a First Class Life.* s.l.: s.n.

Godin, S. (2018). *This is Marketing: You Can't Be Seen Until You Learn to See.* London: Penguin.

Guillebeau, C. (2016). *Born for This: How to Find the Work You Were Meant to Do.* London: Macmillan.

Halbert, B. (2016). *The Halbert Copywriting Method Part 111: The Simple, Fast, & Easy Editing Formula That Forces Buyers to Read Every Word of Your Ads.* California: CreateSpace Independent Publishing Platform.

Hogshead, S. (2014). *How the World Sees You: Discover Your Highest Value Through the Science of Fascination.* New York, NY: HarperCollins.

Keller, G. and Papasan, J. (2014). *The One Thing: The Surprisingly Simple Truth Behind Extraordinary Results.* UK: John Murray.

McKeown, G. (2014). *Essentialism: The Disciplined Pursuit of Less.* UK: Ebury.

Miller, D. (2017). *Building a Story Brand: Clarify Your Message so Customers Will Listen.* USA: HarperCollins Leadership.

Murray, J. (2016). *Your Press Release is Breaking My Heart: A Totally Unconventional Guide to Selling Your Story in the Media.* California: CreateSpace Independent Publishing Platform.

Ries, E. (2011). *The Lean Startup: How Constant Innovation Creates Radically Successful Businesses.* New York, NY: Portfolio/Penguin.

Websites

asa.org.uk (last accessed 28th August 2019)

britishchambers.org.uk (last accessed 28th August 2019)

cisco.com/c/en/us/solutions/collateral/service-provider/visual-networking-index-vni/white-paper-c11-741490.html#_Toc532256789 (last accessed 28th August 2019)

easigrass.com/news/owning-the-most-amazing-car-around/ (last accessed 28th December 2019)

fsb.org.uk (last accessed 28th August 2019)

google.com/business (last accessed 28th August 2019)

gov.uk (last accessed 28th August 2019)

guiseleyosteopaths.co.uk/stans-life/ (last accessed 28th December 2019)

hse.gov.uk (last accessed 28th August 2019)

ico.org.uk (last accessed 28th August 2019)

londonist.com/london/transport/in-pictures-the-best-thought-of-the-
    day-messages-from-the-tube (last accessed 28th December 2019)
ons.gov.uk (last accessed 28th August 2019)
princes-trust.org.uk (last accessed 28th August 2019)

ACKNOWLEDGEMENTS

This book has been a longer journey than I could ever have imagined and without the support of my amazing family and friends, it would never have happened. It has been a huge team effort!

A big thank you to...

Gary, my husband and best friend, for holding the fort while I worked away at the end of the garden—you are my world! Not forgetting our fur family, Bella and Fawkes, I am sorry you missed out on walks and adventures because of me working late—I will make it up to you!

Lisa for your council and fresh take on the book in the days running up to the deadline. Thank you for your insights on professional practice and helping me get across the finish line—you have been amazing!

Siobhan for your tireless proofreading and editing of the original draft, you have the patience of a saint—you are a star!

Ros for your belief in me and drawing the lovely character illustrations that have made numerous appearances in my business throughout the years.

Judy for your hospitality, kindness, and friendship.

Jenny for being my business buddy and keeping me accountable.

All the practitioners I have worked with, learnt from, and taught.

All my clients who have shown me the possibilities.